M. BASIL PENNINGTON, O.C.S.O.

The Manual of Life

*The New
Testament
for Daily Living*

Paulist Press
New York ◇ Mahwah

Photo Credits

Thomas Ackerson, 90, 96; Craig Callan, 106; Paul S. Conklin, 23; Vivienne della Grotta, 20; Marjory Dressler, 11, 15, 26, 35, 39, 55, 58, 76, 112, 117; Dale G. Folstad, 72; Sedge LeBlang/Paulist Fathers, 47; Gene Plaisted, 101; Religious News Service, 42, 64, 79, 83; Paul M. Schrock, 88, 92; Vernon Sigl, 110; Rick Smolan, 52.

Copyright ©1985 by Cistercian Abbey of Spencer, Inc.

Library of Congress
Catalog Card Number: 85-60291

ISBN: 0-8091-2710-5

Published by Paulist Press
997 Macarthur Boulevard
Mahwah, N.J. 07430

Printed and bound in the United States of America

A short time ago a friend gave me one of those wonderful new watches. It is a calculator and a game, it awakens me with a choice of three tunes, it tells me what day it is, it chimes the hours and reminds me of all my appointments. And it bristles with little buttons that control all of this. Happily, it was accompanied with a little booklet which explained all the functions and told me which button to push to get the result I want. I could, of course, have been a know-it-all, and have tossed the little booklet away, saying, "I can figure it out for myself." And I would probably still be trying to figure out how to keep the alarm from going off at 2 A.M.

Far more complex than any digital watch, or any other great invention of the human mind, is the mind itself, the person who has invented all of these. The human person is the most sophisticated product in all creation, and made for the most wonderful of all things: to be unendingly happy and fulfilled with God. "The glory of God is man fully alive," said Augustine. Fortunately, the Maker has given us a book so that we will know how to operate and to achieve what we want. Unfortunately, we are all too prone to throw the book aside or simply to forget it, and set about trying to figure things out for ourselves. And then we wonder why we have such a difficult time coming up with the formula for lasting happiness.

At first reading we might wonder how the Bible is a relevant rule book for human happiness. It is full of stories and some of them are not the happiest. We need to know how to read the Bible. If, reading the instructions for my digital watch, I did not know left from right nor how to count, the booklet I received would not have helped me much. Someone had to have taught me these basics. Knowing them, I easily got from the book how to operate my watch.

The Fathers of the Church, wise men of old, following the example of the inspired Paul, have taught us how to read the Bible as the manual of life. They have taught us that within the literal sense, there is another sense, a spiritual sense, which is multiple. The bright skin of the orange tells us what it is, but it is only when we peel away the rind that we can be nourished. Just as within man there is a spirit which enlivens all we see, so beneath the literal sense of the Scriptures is a spiritual sense which enables them to be a life-giving word for us, nourishing our lives. The Fathers usually distinguished three different spiritual meanings. There is the meaning which reveals the mystery that God wishes to convey to us through the words of the narrative. This the Fathers called the allegorical or figurative sense. Then there is the meaning that speaks of *our* response to this mystery, the moral sense. And finally there is a foreshadowing of the fullness to which all this leads, and this is called the anagogic sense.

1

Saint Paul in writing to the Galatians speaks of Abraham's two wives, Sarah and Hagar, and goes on to say: "These things may be taken figuratively (allegorically), for the women represent two covenants"—the successive conventual relationships into which God has called his people. Paul goes on to speak of Jerusalem. Literally Jerusalem is a city in Palestine. But allegorically it is the community of those gathered into the Church. Morally, it is that communal bonding or gracious favor that makes us one people. Ultimately or anagogically it is "the Jerusalem that is above [that] is free, and she is our mother." It is through these spiritual meanings that the narrative texts of the Scriptures speak to our lives and serve us as a manual of life.

The Gospels and the writings of the Apostles do contain many direct and clear instructions for life. These pages will seek to place these instructions in context. More often they will endeavor to unwrap the spiritual senses that lie within the narrative portions. In all they seek to help make the New Testament a true Manual of Life for you.

I certainly do not want to leave anyone with the idea that the literal sense of the Scripture Text can be overlooked. It has fundamental importance. The spiritual senses rest on it, but we do not want to rest there. In my comments I will seek to put each book of the New Testament in context grounding myself on the latest and best scholarship available. But most of the reflections I will be sharing with you will seek to bring out the meanings of the text which bear most immediately on our everyday lives. Jesus when he spoke to the people did not seek to make them scholars or theologians; he wanted to speak to their hearts and guide them on the way of life. So, too, Peter and Paul and the other inspired writers. The texts I have commented on here are relatively few. As one great spiritual teacher wrote: What page, what word of the Old and New Testament is not a most true norm for human life? (Saint Benedict of Monte Cassino) May these pages inspire you to seek for yourself each day the deeper meanings of the Sacred Text as daily food, as a guide for the journey, knowing that you have been given here a most sure Manual of Life.

True Greatness

Text: Matthew 1:1–16

Did you know that my thirteenth great-grandfather was Lord Mayor of London? And my twelfth great-grandfather married William Penn's step-daughter and brought the family to America? We like to harken back to our ancestry, our roots, especially if it is special, if it gives us distinction.

"Abraham was the father of Isaac, Isaac the father of Jacob . . ." Jesus' pedigree is all laid out for us, from generation unto generation—three times fourteen generations. Matthew's Gospel, as we hear it, is not the oldest of the four but it is based on an earlier text, one written in Aramaic, the language Jesus himself spoke. This Matthew was a man of the Chosen People. It was important to him, as to all the early Jewish Christians, that Jesus is indeed the promised son of Abraham, Jacob and Jesse, and of the great King David. He is of the royal house, the Lion of Judah, the fulfillment of all the prophecies. Again and again we will see Matthew quote the Old Testament and indicate how Jesus fulfills the text.

In the autobiography of Thomas Merton, one of the greatest spiritual masters of our century, there is a very remarkable passage. As a zealous young convert, Merton was going to be the best. He joined the strictest religious Order in the Church, the Trappists. He was elitist. Then one day, while he stood waiting on a street corner in Louisville, he was enlightened. He suddenly realized what a good thing this human race is: "I went through the city, realizing for the first time in my life how good are all the people in the world and how much value they have in the sight of God." With all his heart he thanked God for making him a human.

It may have been important to Jews who honestly were searching the Scriptures for the way of salvation and looking for the Messiah to know that Jesus came from the tribe of Judah and the house of David. It was a fact not easily established because his true link is through his Mother and genealogies were in the male line. (It is worth noting that Matthew does bring four significant women into Jesus' genealogy, three of whom were notable sinners and the fourth a foreigner.) On his Father's side his precedents were the best; he is the very Son of God. But Jesus did not speak of this. When others spoke of it he did confirm it. But, for his part, he constantly affirmed his humanity, calling himself the "Son of Man." He fully, lovingly, and compassionately immersed himself in our humanity and became the hope-giving head of our race.

Our greatness does not lie in being the thirteenth great-grandson of the Lord Mayor of London or in being the Lord Mayor himself or the President of the United States, or the author of best sellers, or a Pope or a physicist, banker or king. Our greatness lies in being a member of the human race, in being a human person made in the very image of God, partaker of his divine nature. More—by baptism we are in fact one with the very Son of God. That is true greatness.

Welcome, Dreamers

Text: Matthew 1:18ff

The first pages of the different gospels are full of vocation stories: Mary, Joseph, John the Baptist, the Apostles, and Jesus himself.

Mary and Joseph had undoubtedly made a long and careful discernment in regard to their very special vocation to live a virginal married life. And they had taken the first step to embark upon it, pledging themselves to each other in the betrothal ceremony. Then suddenly there was an unexpected complication. God sent the best of vocation directors to Mary, one of his own mighty counselors, the angel Gabriel. Mary had only to listen, question, and assent to this amazing new dimension of her virginal vocation—to be the virginal mother of God's own Son.

But Joseph wasn't so immediately favored. In anguish he discerned as best he could. Maybe he failed because he did not consult—but whom could he have consulted? He did the best he could, and God did not let him down. When we do our best, God will do the rest. God did then send an angel to Joseph—in a dream.

In discerning God's will in our lives, in discerning the way in which we are to live out our lives as Christ persons, we need always retain a certain flexibility. Humility calls for this, for we must be aware that we can make mistakes. It is also true that God sometimes leads us step by step—otherwise the first step might seem too big for us. If the first decision we make in regard to our vocation is the right one—good. We are all set and need but faithfully follow our course. But if it

4

proves otherwise, we need to be willing to reconsider, and not give up seeking to follow the Lord. If something wholly unforeseen comes up, it can cause a good bit of anguish (Can you imagine Joseph's anguish!), but humbly, prayerfully we want to go on seeking and courageously making new decisions.

But what about dreams? Should we really take them seriously and expect God to speak to us through them? We cannot deny that God can lead men in this way. Here in the Scriptures we see him doing this again and again. It seems fitting that men like the Magi should have been led by dreams. God seems to meet us where we are and lead us gently forth from there. For some persons, dreams are very significant. They remember them and draw a great deal from them. For such persons it would not be surprising that God might use their dreams to help them in their vocational discernment. But such guidance must be carefully tested, even when it gives a certain inner assurance. Does the dream conform to reality? Joseph's did—Mary had truly conceived of God. Does the dream foster the fruits of the Spirit: love, joy, peace, kindness, gentleness, self-control?

Whether it comes by dreams or by the more normal ways of attraction, insight, and spiritual guidance, we do want to be attentive to the call of the Lord, seek to discern it clearly, and courageously follow it, so that we, too, can fulfill our role in salvation history.

Matthew: Looking for Something New

Text: Matthew 2:6

We call this book the "New Testament," so there must have been an "Old Testament." At the head stands a proclamation of good news, a gospel, by a man who found not enough in the old and wanted something new. He knew the promise of the old—this is everywhere evident in his proclamation—but there seemed to be no new one coming when he was young, no true living hope among his people, no teachers with promise. So he sought something "new" in the promises of the materialistic society that was mastering the world. Matthew accepted the promises of Roman materialism and became its servant, collecting its due—"Render unto Caesar the things that are Caesar's. . . ."

Then one day a Teacher came, and he proclaimed something new—"No man has ever spoken as this man speaks"—and immediately at this Teacher's beckoning Matthew left the "new" that hardly satisfied his deepest longings. As he followed Jesus he discovered, again and again, in the details of his life and mission, the fulfillment of the old, and he noted all this for us.

Well, then, does Matthew's good news stand at the beginning of the New Testament as a passage from the Old, proclaiming its fulfillment?

It is a good starting place for us, too. For Matthew, like so many of us, not finding in the religious experience (or lack of it) of his youth a source of life and hope, turned to the powers of this world. And by the standards of that world he was doing well and should have been quite satisfied. He had his "friends," his wealth, a secure income. He could throw a big party when he wanted. But—something was lacking. Maybe it was the religion of his youth that had planted the hope. It was deeply written in his very nature.

Take up the gospels. Listen with the inner ear, with the deepest longings of your heart exposed—those longings you hardly dare admit to even yourself. And see if the Teacher who here proclaims a new way, a way of love, and seals the testamentary covenant with his blood, does not offer a way that will fulfill all those deepest longings.

We may not all be sons and daughters of Abraham by blood and so share expectations woven deeply in the flesh and in a people of a messianic promise to be fulfilled, an expectation that leads Matthew to trace out a genealogy and prophecies. But we are all children of Adam and there is written in our collective memories and in our flesh the need of a redeemer, a new Adam, a new start for our race. Let us listen attentively and discover that Matthew's Messiah is also our savior, the Savior of the World.

Lord, Teach Us To Pray

Text: Matthew 6:9ff

We are all very familiar with the Lord's Prayer. We have said it—I almost said, rattled it off—many times. We tend to think of it as a prayer formula which we simply repeat. But here in the heart of his most basic teaching, Jesus is teaching us his disciples how to pray. The Lord's Prayer is a school of prayer. It articulates the deepest desires and aspirations that flow out of the human spirit that has been made one with Christ in baptism.

First we are invited to get in touch with who we really are—namely, one who has been baptized into Christ, made son with the very Son. And so our whole being cries out: *Father!* "We do not know how to pray as we ought, but the Spirit who has been poured out into our hearts cries, '*Abba,* Father.' "

But no one of us is an only child. That same generous adoptive love has made us one of many brethren, and so we must always pray: *Our Father.* We do not stand alone before God.

And realizing the immense paternal goodness of God, praise is due: *Hallowed be your name.*

The response to such goodness, such kindness, can only be love. And love expresses itself in unity of wills, in wanting what the Beloved wants: *Your kingdom come, your will be done*—yes even here on earth, with the same perfection and fullness with which it is done in heaven.

And what is God's will? What is the meaning of the whole creation project? Our happiness. God made us to know him so that we might love him, so that we might be happy with him, share in his happiness. God had all happiness, all goodness. But in the supereminent goodness of his love he wanted others to share it with him. And thus he created—he created us, you and me.

But first we must live: *Give us today our daily bread.* Out of the universal compassion that comes from knowing our oneness in the creative source of the Father's love, this cry rises for all the hungry of the earth. But even as we pray in a heartfelt way for the material bread that will sustain human life, we also sense a need and pray for other breads: the Bread of the Scriptures, the Word of Life that feeds our minds and hearts. And we hunger, too, for the supersubstantial Bread of the Eucharist.

We need, too, to live in peace, in peace with ourselves, being at peace with God, and in peace with our fellows: *Forgive us our debts, as we also have forgiven our debtors.*

And lead us not into temptation, but deliver us from the evil one. How often, coming to this phrase, have I experienced the tensions, the strivings, the concerns of life falling away. His is the kingdom. All is within his domain. "He's got the whole wide world in his hands." I need fear nothing. All is under control.

Once an old sister asked St. Teresa: "How can I become a contemplative?" The saint replied: "Say the 'Our Father,' but take an hour to say it." We may not often be able to take an hour to say the Lord's Prayer, but if we really want to learn to pray, it is good occasionally to take time with the Lord's Prayer and let each phrase open out within us and give voice to the deep longings that the Spirit has planted in our hearts. Prayer is not difficult. It is something we deeply long to do.

We need but give it time. Therein lies the difficulty: to make time in our busy lives to do what we really want to do.

Waiting

Text: Matthew 11:2ff

Waiting—how much of our lives is spent in waiting! Indeed, if we are in touch with the deeper inspirations of our being, we realize that all our life is a waiting. We are made for something greater than this world. Nothing here fully satisfies. Some of the saints have spoken of this world as a prison, and they might not be so far from wrong.

John the Baptist's life was one marked by waiting. First he had to wait in the womb. For even in the womb it was given to him to discern the Lord and something of his mission to proclaim him. "As soon as the sound of your greeting reached my ears, the baby in my womb leaped for joy" (Lk 1:44).

And then there were the years in the desert, where he was led by the Spirit to prepare for his mission—some thirty years of waiting. Finally the day came, and he prepared the way of the Lord and pointed him out to those who were to become the Lord's first disciples. But it was a short day. And soon the Baptizer was in prison, again waiting—waiting to see the fulfillment of what he was sent to proclaim. Those were dark days for him. There was nothing more he could do, but wait. He heard little; he longed to see. He sent his disciples questioning.

Our lives are a waiting from the moment of our conception when our human potential begins to seek and wait for its fulfillment. Baptism brings us into a new and higher mission, and we long for its fulfillment. Our daily lives are filled with activities all of which seek their fulfillment. And we have our dark moments and days when we ask ourselves: Does it all add up? Are we really in touch with the true meaning of life? We look to Christ and ask with John and his disciples: "Are you the one . . .?"

And our answer in such times of darkness and questioning lies in the same place as those disciples were to find it: in the witness of the life, the deeds, and the words of Jesus. If we want to keep in touch with the true meaning of our lives, we need each day to search the Scriptures. We need to read the gospels and find

9

there the ultimate meaning we seek, the meaning that gives meaning to all else, the meaning that not only makes the waiting bearable and worthwhile, but that transforms it and fills it with expectant joy.

Take ten minutes each day—who cannot find ten minutes in a day? Take up this Book of Life with reverence and love. Call upon the Holy Spirit to make it a living Word for you. Then for those few minutes listen to your Lord. Let him give you a "Word of Life" that you can carry with you through the rest of the day. Or choose one for yourself from the text you read. Then thank the Lord for his presence in your life in these Scriptures and carry that word with you as a leaven. Repeat it when you can; let it rest in your memory, in your heart. Let it be a love word that makes your Beloved present and that promises you that his love for you will be fulfilled, in an embrace beyond all imagining. And you will wait for him in joyful expectation.

Happiness consists in knowing what you want and knowing that you have it or are on the way to getting it. Happiness is waiting for your Beloved who will surely come (Rev 22:20).

Learning the Hard Way

Text: Matthew 17:24–26

Peter is a great consolation to us. He is so like us. He really loves our Lord. But he is always putting his foot in his mouth—saying things he afterward regrets. All with good will—and perhaps a bit of human respect, too. Here he is quick, too quick to respond to an implied slur on his Master.

How patient Jesus is, and what a sense of humor. He doesn't jump on Peter, or reprimand him. He gently leads him to the realization of his folly and then lets him stew a bit in his own juices. Peter the great fisherman, one of the best on the Sea of Galilee—later we will hear of him pulling in a hundred and fifty-three large fish in a single catch—must go down to the lakeside and cast in a solitary little hook and wait for a solitary little fish. We can well imagine that his eleven cronies did not let the irony of the situation escape notice!

Our Lord respects us. He does not treat us as helpless infants. He has given us minds and hearts, a way of life and spiritual insight. He expects us to use our

gifts to lead a good and happy life. But, so often, as in the case of Peter, human respect, defensiveness, trying to do things our own way or write our own formula for happiness, brings upon us unhappy consequences. God does not shield us from these. He lets us experience them so that we will learn.

We don't know what thoughts went through Peter's mind as he stood on the seashore with his little line waiting for that special fish. He may have had some unkindly thoughts about his taunting confreres. He might even have been tempted to mutter a bit against his Lord. But I suspect our Lord left him there long enough to quiet down and look within himself, and, with a little insight, make some resolves in regard to a wiser future.

"Yes, Yes," and "No, No" or Is It "Yes"?

Text: Matthew 21:28ff

We all know someone like that second son, the one who says right away "yes" but never carries through. They are the worst sort of friends. They really leave us with a feeling of being let down. And yet they are so nice. How can we be angry with them?

We are much happier with the first type, and so is God. Perhaps we are a little like that ourselves. Anyone who is a thinker, who has a mind of his own—a God-given mind—isn't always ready to jump to it at another's command. We want to think about it a bit. Perhaps our pride enters in. We want to be our own person. Our independence asserts itself. Our first instinct is to say "no." We might tend to give people a hard time, and God, too. From what he says here, it seems God doesn't mind that. He understands us. He much prefers our sincerity and honesty.

God himself once sweat blood and agonized over a paternal command. "Father, if it be possible, let this chalice pass from me." But in the end: "Father, not my will, but thine be done."

Jesus said, "He who loves me keeps my command." He didn't say, "He who loves me keeps my command easily." We have all failed—Jesus here speaks of the prostitutes and men who oppressed the people. The question is the bottom line; in the end do we do what we see God wants us to do?

There was a popular play and movie some years ago called *Fiddler on the Roof*. It was the story of a rough and tough old Jewish peasant. If he knew nothing else, he knew there is a God. This peasant had a mind of his own and it wasn't always God's mind. And he didn't hesitate to tell God so. He would shake his fist at the heavens and shout at God. But in the end God would have his way. God loved the peasant and the peasant loved God.

We shouldn't then be surprised if we have found ourselves slow to say "yes" to God, and even at times have said "no." He understands. But now is the time for a courageous "yes." Let us be about our Father's business.

What Is He Saying?

Text: Matthew 25:14ff

God became man, completely human. He got right down into our world, our lives. God became man so that he could be our friend, so that we could be his friends. As a friend he wanted to share with us his thoughts and ideas, his way of seeing things. This is part and parcel of human friendship. In this case, though, since our Friend is God, the source of all wisdom and knowledge, our maker who really knows what makes us tick, and what is our true way to fulfillment and happiness, his friendly sharing has unlimited value for us.

In his accommodating humanness our God-Friend shares his thoughts through very human little stories which we have come to call parables. They are usually very straightforward little narrations with which we can readily identify. Yet, oftentimes they have a sudden twist to them that challenges us and should set us to thinking, seeking to understand the special insight our Friend-Teacher is sharing with us.

The story Matthew recounts in the middle of his twenty-fifth chapter is typical of Jesus' parables. We who have grown up in a capitalistic society can readily understand the wealthy person who underwrites talented men. That the men should make gains commensurate with the capital they received to work with is to be expected. And we readily go with the condemnation of the man who didn't make any profit, especially in the light of his rather ungracious remarks about his underwriter. He deserves to be tossed out of the corporation.

But then there is the twist—or is it a twist? His thousand is handed over to the one who already had the most. What is Jesus trying to tell us here? How does it apply to you, to your life?

The Naked Observer

Text: Mark 1

The gospels are filled with many minor characters who pass on and off the scene, forming part of the living background. One of them is "a young man, wearing nothing but a linen garment," who when seized fled away naked, leaving his garment behind (14:51). This curious detail written into Mark's narrative of the apprehension of Jesus in the Garden has led writers to speculate that this was Mark himself. They further identify him with John Mark, in whose home the early Christians of Jerusalem gathered (Acts 12:12). This may well have been the scene of the Last Supper and account for the presence of Mark in the Garden when the supper party retired there.

It is fun putting pieces together when history has left us few clues. The fact that Peter went directly to Mark's home when he was miraculously delivered from prison (it was really the home of Mary, the mother of John also called Mark—Luke in Acts makes an obvious effort to bring Mark into his narrative) indicates some special connection between the two. But even without this fact, in reading Mark we get a sense of this being Peter's gospel. It has Peter's sharpness and conciseness. It has so many little details which only a few could have known, Peter among them, and which would have stuck in Peter's memory because of the special significance they would have had for him. Peter's failures are clearly set forth, while some of his more glorious moments are left to the other evangelists to relate. Yet the hinge point of Mark's account remains Peter's resounding declaration: "You are the Christ" (8:29). In any case Mark or his source was an observer close at hand, close enough to be seized with Jesus in the Garden had he not eluded grasping hands.

Mark's narrative has long been considered the oldest account of Jesus' life, though that has been questioned by some recent scholarship. It has been believed that the other evangelists had it in hand, thus accounting for some of the very close similarities. If that is the case, the differences are even more important, for they

14

15

are deliberately introduced to throw further light on the account. Read Mark. Enjoy the fast-moving narrative. Then fill it out with the other two that surround him.

On the Inside

Text: Mark 4:21–34

Each night as I settle down for the night, before I go to sleep I read one of G.K. Chesterton's fascinating Father Brown stories. The pattern is always the same. The delightful little priest in characteristic bowler, preceded by his oversized pipe, comes walking into a picturesque scene soon to be besmirched by crime and intrigue. The whole affair is laid out before me and I eagerly await the moment when I will be let in on the inside of the mystery.

As intriguing as any mystery story and more is the mystery of life. We want to understand ourselves, the meaning of our lives, how to find happiness and fulfillment. So we turn to our Maker who is Truth, Life itself, and the Way. We listen to him as our Master. And what does he talk about? He talks about lamps, and seed growing, and the seed itself. What has all this got to do with life—my life?

Jesus reveals everything through his word: ". . . for everything I learned from my Father I have made known to you." But with parables "Jesus spoke the word . . . as much as they could understand." If we want to understand all, to enter fully into the mystery of life, to get the inside story, we have to do two things: "When he was alone with his own disciples, he explained everything."

First of all we have to become his own disciple, to enter into the way of discipleship. We have to really accept him as our Master, a teacher whom we trust and whom we want to follow. And as disciples we will want to sit each day at our Master's feet, listening to him, ready to accept what he says and to shape our lives according to it. Daily gospel reading not as a mental exercise but as a living contact with our Master is the first essential.

And then we have to have time alone with him. We may hear the Word of Life solemnly proclaimed at the Eucharist. We may read the Bible together in a study group. But there needs to be a time, a privileged time, each day when we let everything else go for a bit, "go into our room, close the door, and pray to our Father in secret," and commune with his Son, our Brother, Savior, Master, and Friend. "I

16

no longer call you servants because the servant does not know his Master's business. Instead, I have called you friends, for everything that I learned from my Father I have made known to you."

If we want to get the inside story, here is our chance. Don't miss it!

Who Do You Say That I Am?

Text: Mark 8:29

Who do you say that I am?—the deepest question we can ask. It is one that we perhaps hide from, but nonetheless one we must answer if we are ever to find true happiness. No mirror will ever answer it for us. Just try. Only the eyes of a friend, allowed to look deep within, can reflect back to us who we truly are. In his mystery we can see our own. We need someone who understands us, who believes in us, who acknowledges who we really are. And so did Jesus.

Jesus looked into the eyes of his disciples, or rather into the eyes of the one he was to choose as their leader and head: "But what about you? Who do you say that I am?"

"You are the Christ."

This is the turning point of the gospel of Mark. Now that his chosen ones know this, his mission can go forward to bring this good news to all the people.

Flesh and blood had not revealed this to Peter. Peter could not have discovered this by watching Jesus' activity, his coming and going, his daily doings. He had to look deep into Jesus' eyes and enter into Jesus' mystery where he would discover that Jesus and the Father are one. The Father spoke in Peter's heart as he spoke at the Jordan and would speak again on Tabor: This is my beloved Son.

Peter's knowledge would yet have to be clarified and enlightened, freed from any shadow of a false messiah. But Peter had perceived the essential nature of his Friend.

And now Jesus stands before you, in the real presence of the Scriptures. He looks into your eyes and invites you to look into his. And he says: Who do you say that I am?

What do you answer? Who is Jesus for you? And who are you for Jesus? Are you the one who understands Jesus, who acknowledges who he is?

Why This Waste?

Text: Mark 14:3ff

In this time of heightened social consciousness, we are very apt to join the disciples in murmuring: Why this waste? This alabaster jar of very expensive perfume was worth a hundred days' wages, thousands and thousands of dollars. A drop of it would have been sufficient to fill the whole house with its fragrant odor. But this lover did not pour out a drop. She did not pour it all out. She recklessly broke the precious bottle so that it could all gush out upon her Beloved.

Why this waste? Jesus and his faithful evangelists considered this a supremely important part of the good news. We can tell this by the fact that all four evangelists include it in their account, a relatively rare occurrence. And they place it in a supremely important place, just before the account of the ultimate paschal mystery. Moreover they report that Jesus himself said "wherever the gospel is preached in the world, what she has done will also be told . . . in memory of her." And yet we do not even know her name, whether she was Mary of Bethany, Lazarus' sister, or Mary of Magdala or one of the many other sinful women who came to know the healing compassion of the Master.

She is important to the Lord, this unnamed woman. She is important to him in herself—his secret. And she is important to him, because in her anonymity she stands for all those women and men, mostly unknown and hidden, who pour out the precious perfume of their lives upon him. Yes, "the poor you will always have with you." And he who fed them and healed them, taught them and lived with them as one of them will always call forth disciples and followers to do likewise. And yet, at the same time he will invite some to spend their lives to do a "beautiful thing" for him, to pour out their lives in adoration and contemplation of his beauty, lifting us all up to this, reminding us that this is an important dimension of every Christian's life.

We are first of all disciples of Christ; more, we are one with him in the incomprehensible oneness of baptismal grace. If we are able to bring to anyone anything in the way of true teaching, healing, or life-giving ministry, it is because we have first gone to the source and drawn from him. The second commandment is like unto the first. First we are to know him—in a deeply personal way—and love him, and then serve him in ministering to others, ministering to him in others. First, we are to minister to him in himself. The "wasteful" time of contemplation is at the heart of the Church and at the heart of every truly fruitful apostolic life and ministry.

Why this waste? So that we will not forget and fail to put first things first, to put the First Person first in our lives and in our ministry.

Like Us in All

Text: Mark 15:33ff

God asks nothing of us that he did not ask of himself: to be fully human, to know obscurity and daily fidelity, homelessness and poverty, fear and exile, the loss of a loved one in death, family oppression, opposition and betrayal, abandonment and denial, imprisonment and torture, shame and death. Is there anything that can be asked of us that he did not already suffer?

In all he was completely human in his experiences of life. He knew the need of friendship—"I no longer call you servants but friends"—and at times he was refused it—"Will you also go away?" He enjoyed his friends, especially children—"Let them come to me and forbid them not." "I have longed to eat this meal with you." He experienced profound disappointment in the unresponsiveness of people, even friends, and their failure to understand him. When he sat on the hill overlooking Jerusalem and wept, those were not false tears but the expression of a broken heart. And in the end he knew abandonment and betrayal—"Judas, do you betray the Son of Man with a kiss?"

When we look up at Calvary's hill we see a man truly like ourselves and we see summed up in his agonizing body and spirit—"My God, my God, why have you forsaken me?"—all the sufferings any human can ever possibly be asked to bear. And why? Why did God become man and take on himself the totality of our misery, so much of it due to our own sinfulness and stupidity? Why? Because on the third day he would rise again and he wanted us to know that there is absolutely no suffering, no degradation of our humanity that in the end cannot and will not be overcome by the power of his saving grace. No matter how the circumstances of life, the malice of our fellow humans, and our own stupidity and sin put us down, by his grace we can even now in spirit rise above it all—if we exercise the faith, the hope, and the love that we have. And in the end, the ultimate end, we, too, shall rise to unending freedom, dignity, joy and glory, sharing the one fulfilled

19

humanity of the Christ who suffered the deepest of human ignominy and now possesses the summit of human dignity and glory.

If, as we are buffeted by life's miseries, we can keep before our eyes the cross raised on Calvary's hill we can have a compassionate companion ever with us and all the assurance of the empty tomb and the ascension. It is for our taking—the gift of a God who so loves us that he was willing for our sakes to be one with us and to endure all the deepest dregs of human misery. We need never suffer alone. We need never face the darkness of any tragedy without this ray of hope shining through. We have Calvary and the whole Paschal Mystery. We are already in Christ, our head, a risen people.

Text: Mark 16

It was Holy Saturday morning, a clear cold day. A little boy was standing in front of the old Italian tailor shop, his nose pressed hard against the glass. He was taking it all in, the wonderful reconstruction of Jerusalem, with its many buildings, narrow streets, sparkling pools, and pastoral surroundings.

A derelict, stumbling by, was caught by the child's excited attention and stopped for a moment to look on uncomprehendingly. The little boy started pointing out the different places and shared what he had learned about them in Bible class.

There is the Temple—Jesus taught there, and one day he chased out all the cheating traders. And there is the Pool of Siloam—Jesus cured there. There was a man there who had been sick for thirty-eight years and Jesus told him to get up—he was all better.

The derelict reflected: it was over thirty-eight years since he left his home, wife, and child. Wouldn't it be wonderful if he could be healed of his disease of alcoholism?

The little boy pointed to the Upper Room—that is where Jesus had the Last Supper with his disciples and gave them Holy Communion. Jesus is still with us in the Eucharist.

A hope flickered in the weary old heart—the Healer is still with us. Is it possible?

And there is the High Priest's house, and there is the fortress. The boy went on to recount how Jesus was taken in the Garden, mistreated and falsely accused, and given his cross to carry. Finally, he pointed to Calvary—and there Jesus died.

The elderly man walked away, incredibly sad. One who could help and heal had been rejected and killed. What hope is there?

Then he heard little steps come running up behind him. He turned and looked into a shining, excited little face: "Oh, Mister, he rose again!"

═══════════════════════════════════════ **Joyous Luke**

Text: Luke 1

Mark's account of the good news is concise and precise. He gives us a sharp, detailed, fast-moving picture. There is a robustness about it. Matthew presents himself more as the matured wise man, rooting his account deeply in the soil of a living and hopeful tradition. His is a fulfillment.

With Luke the good news erupts in a cascade of joy and movement. Gabriel wings in from heaven with his announcement. Mary flies across the hills of Palestine to sing her *Magnificat:* My soul praises the Lord and my spirit rejoices in God my Savior. Old Simeon sings his *Nunc Dimittis* in peace and a wiser Zachariah breaks out of his silence to praise the Lord.

If Mark is Peter's scribe, there is good reason to believe that Luke turned to Mary as a primary source. He knows that "Mary treasured up all these things and pondered them in her heart." And he draws from this storehouse. He gives the Mother's picture of Jesus' early life, from the first moment of his conception until his first declaration of manhood and mission.

Luke seems to have had a partiality for women. Their role is much more fully portrayed in his gospel. Maybe it was the gentleness of the physician, for he was a doctor by profession. He understood the role of emotions and feelings. He gives us a text filled with feeling and human emotion, whether it be of joy or sorrow, fear or anger. And he gives us a text that is filled with praise from beginning to end: "And they stayed continually at the temple, praising God" (24:53). He is a man of a grateful and joyous heart.

Luke tells us he examined the witnesses carefully. He listened not only to the facts they expressed in their words but to the tone and color that surrounded the words and let all of this flow into his own heart and then into his pen. We could hardly do better than to imitate Luke, listen with him, and let the flow continue into our own hearts until we, too, are filled with the joy of the good news and erupt in unending praise.

Text: Luke 5:1–11

Vocation is a strange sort of thing. We think we are the masters of our own destiny—and we are. We struggle during adolescence to break loose and stand on our own. Then suddenly someone walks into our lives. Peter was washing his nets, a daily task. He didn't expect this day to be any different from yesterday and so many other yesterdays. And then suddenly this special person was sitting in his boat.

Peter listened, along with the rest. He opened himself to the beauty of this other. Then came the challenge: to go apart with this special person, to put out into the deep, to trust, to put aside some of his own ideas and make space for something beyond the ordinary. When we do this, life suddenly becomes very full, full to overflowing.

The person who steps into our lives may be the Lord himself, and the call, a call to intimacy with himself—celibacy for the kingdom. Or it may be the Lord in another human person, and the call, a call to that intimacy we name marriage—a sacrament of human love that tells of God's love for his people and our love for him. Such bondings in love are always fruitful, whether it be in actual children—physical or spiritual—or in other life-creating activity. True love is in community and is fruitful in community, fruitful beyond all expectations.

Unfortunately, one of the reactions we are capable of when true Love enters our lives is to close ourselves to it. It is too much, too good. We know our sinfulness and our unworthiness. At such a moment we need the humility of Peter to blurt it all out so that we can discover we are so loved that all our sin and misery make no difference. If in fear or pride we seek to hide that which we don't like in ourselves (usually we are convinced that if the wonderful person who has come into our lives sees us as we truly are, that person won't love us) we will never really let love in and we will never know how truly lovable we are and how aboundingly fruitful our lives can be.

In the end what it really amounts to is that we do have to let go of everything, all our preconceived ideas and phony self-images, and follow the way of love.

Whether our call is to follow the Lord in the intimacy of celibacy or in the communion of marriage, we need to hear the Lord's words: Don't be afraid. Put out into the deep. Say "yes" to love.

A Desert Bloom

Text: Luke 7:11ff

I have sitting on my window sill a large pot of assorted desert cacti. They are not particularly lovely things—in fact, they are quite ugly. Some of them are just stolid little balls bristling with threatening spikes. Others twist in every distorted direction. Yet I keep them and water them regularly, for I know that someday, perhaps a dark and dreary day when I least expect it, one or another of them will suddenly erupt with a magnificent blossom and fill the room with a most fragrant odor.

At times, perhaps most of the time for some of us, our prayer life seems to be as lifeless and dry as a cactus. Faith, hope, and charity seem far from us. We can only be before the Lord in our misery, dry, empty, needy, yearning. And that is enough.

In the resurrection of the son of the widow of Naim, one of Jesus' greatest miracles, we have just such a case. The sorrow was profound. Here was a poor widow. She had already lost her husband. All she had to depend on for her declining years was her sturdy son. And now that son was suddenly taken from her. The village wept and wailed with her. There was nothing left to her. There is no hope evinced in the story—no indication of even an appeal to Jesus. Misery was there and Mercy came upon it.

The gratuity and the caring love of God shines forth. Even when we were still dead in our sin, he sent forth his Son, the Merciful One, to walk along our roads and raise us to new life. We did not have to ask for it. All we have to do is accept it. The young man had made no appeal for life. No one had made it for him. Yet when Jesus did speak he had to respond and sit up.

We must not let even our apparent "deadness" hold us back from placing ourselves before the Lord. But when at length he does call us forth, let us unhesitatingly respond.

Jesus gave the newly risen son to his mother. When he calls us to the renewed life of grace, he entrusts us to Mother Church. She will care for us. And we in turn are to care for her. Our life in grace, in Christ, is given to us not for ourselves alone but for the Church who has been widowed on Calvary as her Spouse gave his life for her, for us all. Grateful for our life in Christ, we must know it is given for the Church and have a careful concern for the Church and for her mission.

We are entrusted, too, to another Mother, to Mary, Jesus' own Mother. In the ultimate moment of his life he said to each one of us: Behold your Mother. If our life in grace seems frail, challenged as it is in so many ways, let us rely mightily on this Mother who can obtain from her Son all that we will ever need.

It is fun to speculate on the life of the son of the widow of Naim after his resurrection. We wonder what might have been his perspective on life here on earth after having tasted life beyond the grave. Our own renewed life in grace is always filled with promise, expectation, mystery. Walking with God in the fullness of grace, there is no limit to what might happen. Let us open to the wonder of a life with Christ in God. Let the desert cactus bloom.

Text: Luke 13:19

I took a long walk in the woods this afternoon. It had snowed heavily two days ago. Now the melting snow has begun to pack and it is good for walking. As I looked through the stands of naked trees the green pines stood out. Suddenly I became aware of how many little pines there are carpeting the forest floor, some of them just a few inches tall, pushing through the snowy robe of white. I looked at them and wondered: How many of these little ones will have a chance to grow

to their full potential like the towering pines around me standing proudly above the surrounding forest, some fifty or sixty feet tall.

I thought back over the recent years during which I have served as a vocation counselor. I have spoken with hundreds of fine young men. In each was planted a seed of grace, an aspiration, a hope, a question, a call to be someone in the Body of Christ. I wondered how many of them would allow that seed to grow up within them and realize its full potential. The kingdom of God—which is within—"is like a mustard seed, which a man took and planted in his garden. It grew, became a tree, and the birds of the air perched in its branches" (13:19).

I leaned against a great oak. All was silent, unlike the summer when you can always hear the rustling of leaves, the chirping of birds, the squealing of squirrels. I could almost hear the pines growing. "Night and day, whether he sleeps or gets up, the seed sprouts and grows, though he does not know how."

The seed of grace sown in us at baptism quietly grows. We don't know how. But each day it grows if only each day we say "yes" to life, to growth. God speaks to us through the circumstances of each day: the sunshine or the rain, the warmth of joy or the shower of tears. Each is to growth. He speaks to us through friends and fellow growers, some who bless and some who in their hurt seem to curse. We have but to say "yes" to the reality of each, seeing behind each our Father's providence, and with that "yes" growing to divine stature. For we are called to be perfect even as heavenly Father is perfect, letting the rain of his loving compassion fall upon good and bad alike.

Though we do not know how, the seed of grace will grow in us until we have such big branches that we are a support and refuge for all who come our way, if only each day we say "yes" to God.

Holy Ambition

Text: Luke 14:7

There is almost always an unusual twist in Jesus' parables, and there surely is one here in this story of the wedding feast. At first blush we see it as a story about humility and self-effacement. But is it that?

Actually Jesus is not telling us in the final analysis to put ourselves down. For why does he say to choose the last place? To get ahead! It is a bit of Jesus' "simple as doves, but wise as serpents" theology. No one really wants the last place. Those who choose the last seat or pew have other ends in mind. Certainly it would be no tribute to the Lord if one wanted to be as far away from him as possible at his heavenly celebration. John and James were not reproved for having their mother seek to get them the places closest to Jesus in the kingdom. They were asked if they were willing to pay the price. More fundamentally they were reminded that all goodness, precedence, holiness, even the ability to pay the price comes to us from the Father—a gratuitous gift given according to his love.

Saint Benedict says in his Rule: Do not seek to be called holy, but first seek to be holy so that you can be called holy. Maybe that is the key to our Lord's parable here. Be grounded in reality. Don't worry about place, what people say or think. Be free enough to settle down wherever you land and be confident the Lord will get you into the right place—the one he has planned for you from all eternity—and everyone will know it. When you come down to it, it is not the first or the last place that matters but the right place. That is the best place. And that is where the Lord is for us, for God is where his will is.

So we don't have ambitions for the highest place in heaven (actually that is already taken by Mary, "for he that is mighty has done great things for her"). Nor are we to be content to squeak into the last place (unless that is what God wants for us). We want the place Jesus has gone to prepare for us, that place with all its fullness—and nothing less!

Disciples

Text: Luke 14:25ff

Our monastery has an interesting location. To one side of us is a Buddhist meditation center, and to the other there is a Hindu ashram. Happily, we have the best of relations with these communities. Whenever their chosen teachers come, they share their excitement with us. "Satchitananda is coming! Won't you come to hear him? Would you like us to bring him to see you?" They are very proud of their masters and proud to be their disciples.

I often wonder: Why do we not have the same feelings about our Master? After all it was he who made all these other masters. Perhaps it is because his teaching is not so easy to understand and live.

Here he speaks of "hating" father and mother—this preacher of a gospel of love! This is, of course, Semitic exaggeration. It means putting someone in second place. The disciple of Christ must put him in first place. Monks are seen doing this, forsaking family to go to the monastery. The paradox of it is that monks are usually the most loving of sons. Putting Christ first we learn how to be completely self-giving lovers and in turn are able to love everyone more.

But Christ's call and teaching here are not just for monks: "anyone" —everyone—who would be a disciple of Christ must follow this way. To follow Jesus who carried a cross one must carry a cross.

Jesus describes his way here in a couple of curious little parables. He speaks of building and fighting. Following Jesus we build up a kingdom. Following Jesus we have to struggle against the forces of evil in us and in the world. But the key to these parables lies in the final sentence: "In the same way. . . ." The carrying of the cross with which Christ overcomes the powers of darkness and builds up the kingdom doesn't just happen. It requires planning. This is why we need times of retreat—at least an annual period apart. Better, we need a monthly retreat day— to see how things are going and to plan how to muster our forces to keep our lives moving in the direction we want them to move.

There are then two questions we need to ask ourselves: Do I want to be a disciple, or rather whose disciple do I want to be, for in fact we are all disciples? If not Jesus', whose? Some other master's? He made them all. Or do we want to be our own master? Saint Bernard said wisely: he who is his own master is the disciple of a fool.

If we want to be disciples of Jesus, then we must ask ourselves how we are going to go about taking up our daily cross, how we are going to give up everything. Monasticism is one answer, though it is not the common answer. Within marriage, the more common answer, one will perhaps find it in loving care for one's spouse, for children, for aging parents, for those in want with all their different needs. In quiet times apart—finding them can be part of the challenge—seeing our lives in perspective, we need to ask: How would Jesus our Master respond to these life circumstances? And how can I muster my forces to respond his way? In this way we can be his disciples.

Unemployment

Text: Luke 16:1

All too many in our times know what it is to get laid off, with or without cause. Security, respectability, a lifetime's investment suddenly disappear. Phantoms of fear suddenly crowd in. Fears are greatly multiplied when there is question of wife and children. We can then in some way sympathize with this manager, wasteful though he may have been.

He was commended by his former employer—not for his honesty, but for his craftiness. It was perhaps this trait that led to his being hired in the first place, and which had served his employer well. He is commended by his employer, but not by the Lord. By worldly values he did well—but it was only by worldly values and they don't go very far. Or perhaps they go too far—they go straight to hell.

When we are laid off the worries crowd in. It is easy to lose perspective. Let us not be worldly wise but truly wise. The Lord has his solution. Read again Matthew 6:25–34 and see what it is.

As Saint Peter counseled the early Christians in their time of trial: Cast your care upon the Lord, for he has care of you.

Duties

Text: Luke 17:7–10

I was on a trip recently and we stopped at a restaurant for dinner. It was a restaurant which had a very good reputation, so I was looking forward to a fine meal. As we enjoyed our drinks and munchies the waiter took our order and we soon were served nice big crispy salads. The restaurant was living up to its reputation. Then we waited and waited. Finally our waiter arrived with the entree. But the plates were cold and the appearance of the sauce made it quite evident that things had been left standing somewhere for a good bit of time. I was annoyed and made some remark. The waiter said rather apologetically that he had not had time to eat that day, so he took a few minutes to grab a quick bite. His explanation, far from lessening my anger, only increased it. He was supposed to be waiting on us. We were paying good money for his service. He could eat later.

Aha! I saw then for the first time the real meaning of the story our Lord told about the servant. We have duties, whether they arise out of a job we have taken and are getting paid for or out of some other relation. And everyone has a perfectly good right to expect that we will fulfill those duties. We don't deserve any great thanks for that. It is quite simply our duty. And this world and any organization or group in it is going to work only insofar as each does his duty. When we do something beyond the call of duty, then thanks are indeed due. I am not saying it is not a good thing to appreciate others when they do do their duty, and to acknowledge them and thank them. They are doing their bit to keep things going well. But we have every right to expect each to do his duty.

Our Lord reminds us here, then, that we are all servants of the God who created us. He has made us his stewards, to care for his creation. His pay is the highest: unending happiness, care, love, the fulfillment of all our needs and desires for all eternity. But for now, we have a job to do—his will in caring for ourselves, for each other, and for this world he has made for us. It is our side of the contract of life. So we shouldn't be thinking ourselves heroes, or patting ourselves on the back just because we are "good Catholics."

In fact, we may need to stop and take a look and see if we are in truth good Catholics in the way he wants us to be good Catholics. Do we have a true catholic sense, which means "universal"—a universal caring for his creation: each of our brothers and sisters as well as the ecology of his creation? Or are we rather parochial in our catholicism, taking care of our own, fulfilling our duties in home and parish, but at the same time wasting this earth, supporting wasteful policies of our government, enjoying the riches of the earth with little regard for our brothers and sisters in other neighborhoods or other nations?

Our Lord tells us here that we should say, "We are unworthy servants; we have only done our duty." I find that a bit jarring. If I have done my duty, I don't think I am unworthy. What he means is that we are not worthy of particular commendation when we have merely done what is our true duty. If my waiter had brought my meal promptly, as he should have, he would hardly be worthy of particular commendation. That is what we expect a waiter to do. God, who made us, has every right to expect that we will fulfill our duties in creation, and doing that gives us no claim to special commendation. Yet this is the goodness of our God. We will be honored for all eternity for every least service we render. As he has said elsewhere, when we give a glass of water to someone for love of him, it will not go without its reward. As creatures, called out of nothingness, we certainly have no claim on God. He has every right to demand everything from us, for he has given us everything. And yet he gives us our freedom to say "no" to him and promises to reward every instance in which we say "yes" to him. Doing all he asks of us, we will receive our full wage—eternal life—and doing it with a smile we will receive our "tip," shaken together, pressed down, and flowing over—for the Lord loves a generous giver.

Up a Tree—Out on a Limb

Text: Luke 19:2ff

Recently I visited one of our brothers in Memorial Hospital. As I came out of the hospital a parade was passing by. I could hear it but I could not see it, for the hospital is surrounded by a high wall. As I made my way across the parking lot a youngster came sprinting past me. In a moment he was up a tree. The wall did not prevent him from getting a good view of the parade.

I thought of the recent film "Gandhi"—that great march to the sea. I thought of Pope John Paul II in Battery Park, New York, with great crowds pressing to see and seeing little, and the adventurous ones who were willing to climb the trees and see all.

Zacchaeus, the little man, wanted to see Jesus. He might have thought it to be only curiosity, but in fact something more powerful was stirring within him— powerful enough to drive past his ordinary human respect and self-consciousness, powerful enough to drive him up a tree and out on a limb. And his search was rewarded—rewarded by him who had said: Seek and you shall find.

How often do we fail to seek, and therefore to find what we truly want, because we are afraid of making fools of ourselves? People do laugh at serious Christians, those who take Christ seriously and try to live in this world by his rules.

And we fear, too, the consequences. Zacchaeus' desire pushed him on, but he probably didn't realize how exposed he was. He thought the leaves of the tree would well enough conceal him. Can you imagine his consternation when the Master stopped below him and looked right up at him—and then addressed him? Probably no one was as surprised as Zacchaeus himself when he heard himself saying: "I give half of my possessions to the poor, and if I have cheated anybody out of anything, I will pay back four times the amount." When we risk and give Jesus half a chance, we suddenly find ourselves pushed beyond our supposed limits. We find new freedom to be the person we really want to be. What freedom Zacchaeus found in that moment from the riches that had chained him all his life.

The Lord is always passing by. We have to have the courage to rise above our daily doings, and to put ourselves at risk—to get out on a limb. We do this by taking time, letting things go for a bit; we sit quietly with the Lord, and listen to him, first in the Scriptures and then in the depths of our own being at the center. "Be still and know that I am God." Then we can perceive that the Lord is indeed looking at us. And in the power of that communication of love he can call us forth to a hitherto unknown freedom to be who we truly want to be.

JOHN

Text: John 1

If we have read through the other three gospels we have had the sense of three witnesses describing the same events from different vantage points. There is no doubt they are telling the same story. According to their natural gifts, their sources, and the leading of the Spirit they have brought out different details, emphasized different aspects. As we read one after the other we feel enriched. The story is filled out. Our hearts' desire to know more and more about Jesus is being fulfilled.

But John comes as a bit of a shock. It is as though while the others survey the scene from north, south, east and west, John soars above and even wings his way into the eternal origins of the God-Man. Tradition has rightly symbolized John as an eagle. The disciple whom Jesus loved, the one who could lean back and rest his head on Jesus' bosom and hear the beating of his heart (13:23), certainly had a privileged vantage point. He knew that if the whole story were to be told "even the whole world would not have room enough for the books that would be written" (21:25). So he chose those vignettes that for him allowed one to grasp the essential mystery of the Word become flesh.

John's gospel then calls for a different reading. The main lines of the human story of Jesus have been learned from the three Synoptics, as Matthew, Mark, and Luke are sometimes called. With John we are rather invited to pause for a bit and penetrate more deeply, to look back into the eternal origins, to look forward to coming mysteries (John's second book, Revelation, will treat more of this) and to look now into the meaning of the Eucharist, divine friendship, and an intimacy that partakes of the very unity of the Trinity: "That all of them may be one, Father, just as you are in me and I am in you" (17:21).

Of all the books of the New Testament this is the one we will most want to abide with in prayer, letting John lead us into the very depths of Christ's heart where he will make known to us everything he has learned from his Father (15:15). John's gospel is a call to divine friendship.

Sharing = Sufficiency +

Text: John 6

This was his big day. He was one of the thousands who had followed the Master around the lake. There was enough excitement in that—that he was allowed to go along. His mother had taken care to see that he was provided for, but he was allowed to go along with the older ones in this excited following, to see the Master and perhaps witness some of his wonders. But now. . . . One of the Master's chosen ones had come to him and was now leading him through the reclining crowd to the Master himself.

He clutched his precious little basket of food. He was hungry enough and there wasn't all that much there—and one didn't know how long this would all go on. Nonetheless, when he looked into the face of the Master—he would never forget that look, nor would he ever attempt to describe it —he immediately knew what was wanted. The Master wanted his few loaves and fishes, or rather he wanted him to share them with others. It would have been easy enough to give them to the Master—that would have been special enough to make the sacrifice and live with his grumbling stomach, suddenly aware of how empty it was—but to share with all these strangers! Besides what was so little with so many? Yet it was clear. The Master wanted him to give all, and to strangers: whatever you do to the least, you do to me.

He gave, brave little man, and he learned the great lesson of life. It is more blessed to give than to receive. More: in giving we receive far more than we give. And this day it was so literally true.

The Master took his little gift, and he said thanks—thanks to him and thanks to the Father, the source of all that is. And then the Master began breaking the bread and handing it out. And he kept handing it out, and he kept handing it out, and he kept handing it out. The little man received all he could eat and so did all around him, and indeed all the thousands there. And the same thing happened with the fish. What a celebration!

How different it would have been if he had insisted on hoarding his little supply. He would never have eaten so well himself. And sure enough, soon a hungry adult would have been pulling at his basket. Then others. There would have been scrapping over the scraps. A few would have angrily eaten a stolen morsel. No one would have been filled. Anger and jealousy and hatred would have been fomented.

Is not this the story of our world? Repeatedly presidential studies and United Nations' studies have affirmed that there are more than enough food supplies in this world of ours. Our provident Father is ever ready to multiply seed to feed the nations. Yet those who have cling to the little they have. They hoard for tomorrow while brothers and sisters in other parts of the world go hungry. Their own future prosperity is more important to them than the very life of others. And then they wonder why the world greets them with suspicion and hatred, why there is strife among the nations.

One could wonder what would have happened if the little boy had held back four of his loaves and agreed only to share one with this hungry crowd. But the Lord asked from him more than his loaves. He asked for an attitude, an attitude of sharing all. Only then will there be sufficient for all.

The attitudes of nations are formed in the hearts of the people. We don't have to wait until we can turn a nation around. In the end it is the Lord who performs the miracle of feeding the multitude. And he can begin with the least but total offering. We can respond today and share what little we have with those around us and then leave the rest to the Lord. And in the giving we will discover that we are enriched in ways we never expected. We may not come home with twelve basketfuls (I wonder what the little fellow did with them!) but we may come home with an expanded heart that is filled with something far more precious than bread. And in a most powerful way we will be saying to the Lord that we are ready to do our share so that he may feed all his children here on earth.

The Ideal Community (?)

Text: John 13

Jesus had said: "I have eagerly desired to eat this meal with you." It was a most special night, a most special meal. It was to be the climactic moment in his relationship with these chosen men. He was to open to them as never before the depths of his heart. And he was to go further and give them that very heart, the whole of his flesh and blood.

He had chosen the place. He sent Peter and John, his chosen leader and the "disciple whom he loved," to prepare things. How much he wanted this to be a perfect evening for them. For he knew what lay in store. And yet. . . .

Can you imagine his instinctive reaction as they entered the room and the twelve started their old squabble over who should take precedence. How hard he had tried to teach them. Remember the parable about the marriage feast and the first place? But more by example: Learn of me, for I am meek and humble of heart. Again he would try. And he set about the servant's task, serving them, washing their grimy feet.

This was his chosen band, his ideal community, the bedrock for his Church. And still it was rife with ambition and contention, and even betrayal: One of you will betray me.

And yet he did not walk out on them. He would take this motley crew of all too human men and unite them now in a banquet of love. He would pray for them: that they may be one, even as he is one with the Father. Were not all his parables about his Church, his kingdom on earth, the story of weeds in the wheat, of good fish and bad all mixed together?

37

Is there an "ideal Christian community"? The Christian community is certainly one with ideals, but it is also one that is very realistic. Jesus knew what is in man. He came as a healer, for sickly sinners. It would be these who would form his "ideal" community. And so he would put up with squabbling disciples, yes, even with traitors. He would love them, he would never cease reaching out to them, inviting them, showing them a better way, and never giving up on them.

Christians should not be surprised to find sinners in the Church, indeed, to find sin in their own lives. Like the disciples, we need but allow the Lord to wash us again and again, and to nourish us with his Body and his Blood. Then we can hope that like the eleven, in the end we can return love for love, life for life, and form part of that ideal community in heaven.

We Must Be Clipped

Text: John 15:1

Yesterday Bob, my friend from Texas, visited me. It is late fall now. All the leaves are gone from the trees and vines. It is cold and damp; the chill eats right through to the bone.

My friend has a prize-winning vineyard on the edge of the escarpment above Houston. He is known throughout Texas for his expertise. I have a few vines out behind the shed. So we went out to see them, pruning shears in hand.

I remembered the glory of these vines just a short time before. Golden grapes in abundance hung in large clusters, set off by the leaves that had taken on all the brilliant hues of a New England fall. Now the twisted vines stretched out, naked, dry and gnarled.

Bob started to attack them, it seemed, almost viciously. He cut them back severely. It seemed an unjust reward for their recent fruitfulness. But I had faith in my visitor. I knew this severity would bring only greater fruitfulness when these vines' time of glory comes next fall.

We, too, can look back on our own lives and see that we have done well. We have tried to do all that God has wanted. And the good fruit that has come forth

from our activity confirms that. A tree is to be judged by its fruit. And, yet, how often it happens. After serving so well, we get knocked down and out; everything seems to go wrong. Where's the justice? Where is God in all this?

He is right here, on the job. The most practiced of masters, he has his pruning shears in hand. Skillfully he shapes the events of our lives. Like the vintager who truly loves his vines, the Lord clips us, sometimes in a seemingly savage way, that we might bear much fruit and show ourselves his true disciples. We are the disciples of the Risen One, called to bear fruit unto eternal life—but like him we must first be clipped.

The Questioner

Text: John 21:15ff

I was sitting on the train, reading my Bible. After about a half-hour or so, the woman sitting next to me asked shyly: What are you reading? One question led to another. We soon had a wonderful conversation going.

Most of us like others to ask us questions. We like people to be interested in us, what we are doing, what we think. And we like to ask questions, to get to know others and to learn new things. This is all very natural. It is a wonderful, rewarding experience to go on a walk with a four-year-old. He constantly asks questions. He is never satisfied: why? why? why? And his natural, uninhibited curiosity opens our eyes to the things we have been passing by.

Jesus has been asking questions throughout these gospel texts. Have you noticed? There are some hundred and forty of them. Have you tried answering them? You might find it a most rewarding and enriching experience to go back over the texts and try to answer each of our Lord's questions. It won't be easy. It will call for some deep soul-searching. Answering them, you will get to know better who you are, who he is, and what you mean to each other.

Ultimately Jesus asks us the question he here asks Peter: Do you love me more than these . . . more than everything else?

Can we answer with Peter: "Lord, you know all things; you know that I love you"?

ACTS OF THE APOSTLES

Text: Acts 1

The movie industry has learned it is the road to box office success: take a character who has won the hearts or at least the imaginations of many and bill him again in the on-going adventures of life. We have seen it, not just with good heroes like Rocky or Superman, but with real baddies like the Godfather and even animals like Jaws. It is very natural to want to know more, to want to know what happened next. Where did our hero or anti-hero go from where we last saw him, and what about all those persons around him who equally perhaps worked their way into our hearts?

Luke had "carefully investigated everything from the beginning" (1:3) and in "Luke I" "wrote about all that Jesus began to do and to teach until the day he was taken up to heaven, after giving instructions through the Holy Spirit to the apostles he had chosen" (1:1–2). And then what happened? That's the story of Acts: "Luke II."

It is still the story of Jesus, Jesus now at work in his Body, the Church, in his members, his disciples, and in his vicar. To understand the role of the Church in our lives, to understand the role of the bishops in the Church and of the Pope, Peter's successor, Christ's vicar, we need to read Acts. The first part of Acts is really the Acts of Peter (up to chapter twelve) and then it becomes in substance the Acts of Paul, the other great pillar of the Church.

Acts is an apt transition from the gospels to the epistles or letters of the apostles. Acts places these letters in their context. From Acts we get to know the churches to whom these letters were written, the context in which they were thought out, and even the authors who wrote them. You might find it fruitful as you read Acts to fill out your reading by turning to the respective epistles as the churches or the persons to whom they are addressed emerge from the story.

Luke in a sense provides his own outline of Acts, placing it in the mouth of Jesus. Or it might be truer to say that Jesus' activity in and through his Church progressed as he foretold, and this is what Luke records: "You will be my witnesses

41

in Jerusalem, and in all Judea and Samaria, and to the ends of the earth." We find the Church establishing itself and forming its structures, apostolic leadership and deacons to assist, within the Jewish community at Jerusalem until persecution scatters it abroad. Even then the mission is largely among the Jewish Diaspora, venturing into Samaria, until the "Pentecost" of the Gentiles in Cornelius' house and the mission of Paul to the nations. In the end Peter and Paul reach the center of their civilization and firmly root the Church there by soaking the soil of Rome with their blood and planting their bodies within it.

The whole story is not in Acts. Alongside Scripture there is always the living tradition. We will pick up many strands of it in the epistles. The Scriptures belong to a community. They come out of a community's experience and reflection. It is Acts which puts us in touch with that community in its earliest days, the same community we are part of as members of the Catholic Church.

Different Jobs—All for the Kingdom

Text: Acts 6:2ff

Peter had grown a lot. He had learned something about humble service. The picture had burned itself deep in his mind: the night before he died, the Master kneeling at Peter's feet and washing them. And even as he washed, the Master knew that Peter was to deny him—three times—that very night.

Peter didn't mind serving now, yet there were so many ministries to be attended to. He had to preach—that was first. The Master had commanded: Go forth and teach all. He had to pray: Peter had learned the hard way that he had to pray lest he enter into temptation and prove unfaithful. He had to govern, to lead the growing Church: You are Peter and upon you I will build my Church. Here are the keys of the Kingdom. He had to heal: Peter's very shadow was wiping away all sorts of diseases. But the poor needed attention, too. They needed to be fed, clothed and housed: Whatever you do to the least of mine, you do to me.

It was time to share the ministry.

Feeding, clothing, housing, the care of the poor, administration of the community's goods—these were, in a way, worldly jobs. They required a good bit of practical know-how. Yet they required true virtue: equity, compassion, justice and mercy. The Church must never be just a social agency. The poor and all the membership have a right to expect more. The ministry of care is to be a sacramental presence of the care of God, our Father, who feeds and clothes the sparrows and the lilies of the field and, much more so, his children. So in choosing the candidates for this new level of ministry in the Church it was rightly required that they be persons "who are known to be full of the Spirit and wisdom" (6:3).

Among the people of God there should never be a divorce between the active and contemplative dimensions of life, even if there be different ministries and different emphases in each life. Through prayer and contemplation the deacon and all engaged in active ministry are to come to know God in a deep, personal way, so that when they come to their service they can readily perceive God present in those they serve and bring to them the reverence due. The poor rightly expect something more from the one who comes to minister in the name of Christ and his Church. That something more is an affirmation and reverence that enables the poor person to be in touch with his or her dignity as a child of God, one who shares the divine life. It is this Spirit that leads Mother Teresa of Calcutta to gather up the dying derelicts from the gutters and so care for them that no one ever leaves without his "ticket for heaven." All service, however humble, when it flows out of a contemplative heart, is transformed into ministry for the Kingdom.

Roots

Text: Acts 7

Sometime ago one of the television networks put on a mini-series telling of a black man's search back through slavery and into Africa to find his roots. The series had phenomenal success. It had more viewers than any series ever previously shown. Alex Haley was not alone in his desire to know his roots. We all want to know we are solidly grounded, that we come forth from a people, that our roots sink deep into a living tradition.

If we are going to put our faith in a church, we want to know that it, too, has roots that go deep to the very source of life. Our Church does. Again and again

Acts recounts the sermons of our founding fathers, the apostles, which show that our roots do reach back to the beginning of revelation and the first call of a people. Here, in Stephen's witness we have the longest and fullest account.

But we can't stop at roots or even with what has grown forth from them until now. We must be open to ever new growth.

Stephen's hearers listened so long as he recounted the past, the sort of traditional teaching they were familiar with. But the moment he began to speak in the same spirit of the new, they could not tolerate it.

Jesus said the wise householder brings forth things old and new. The Spirit ever renews his Church. Our roots are precious. They give us a certain security—but we can't stop there. We must be open to the new, be renewed in the Spirit, even if we are stoned like Stephen. Otherwise we might well find ourselves throwing the stones at the true servants of the Master.

Out of the Nest

Text: Acts 12

I was sitting high up, and feeling high. I had been backpacking for days. Today was mostly straight up. I was not far from the summit. But now as I sat in the cool shade of an expansive fir I enjoyed the magnificent panorama that spread out at my feet. I could see for miles and miles. It was a luminously clear day.

Not far from me was a jutting crag that reached up another three hundred feet. As I sat quietly there I suddenly beheld a rare spectacle. A great eagle flew out from her nest hidden in the crag. On her back a little one clung, no doubt, for life itself. Suddenly the mother eagle shook the little one off. It fell helplessly toward the earth, its weak little wings flailing about ineffectively. As the little one plunged, the great mother swooped down and coming beneath caught the little one on her strong broad shoulders and soared triumphantly aloft. The show was repeated again and again; each time the little one gained a little more power and coordination. I am sure if I had been able to stay there long enough I would have witnessed the proud moment when the mother had no need to swoop down—the little one would fly safely under the shadow of her wings.

The infant Church was carried as it were on the shoulders, or, more accurately, the name of the Lord. The proclamation of his resurrection, the signs and wonders worked in his name, the courage of those endowed with his grace was powerfully upholding. Then suddenly Stephen lay in a bloody heap. All their lives were threatened with violence. The little Church plunged down from the Hill of Sion, scattering in all directions to all parts of Judea and beyond, even into the territory of the inimical Samaritans.

But the caring Lord swept down. The Church was reconstituted in towns and villages everywhere in the power of the same Spirit. It would even be carried into Ethiopia.

But again and again violence would lash out. One of the apostles would lose his head. Peter would be thrown into prison. And again and again the Spirit of the Lord would uphold his Church, each time raising it up to go forth yet stronger. Acts traces the path, records the events, the plunges and the ascents, the moments powerful in the Spirit and the moments of faltering humanity. In fact, two thousand years later we still witness the struggle of God's people to take full possession of their divinization.

The story repeats itself in each of our lives, doesn't it? At baptism we come into the divine life. At times the Lord seems to uphold us. All is well. Other moments he seems to disappear, to shake us off. And we plunge. We flail about. Then suddenly he is there again and we soar to new heights. And then again we seem abandoned. But little by little we begin to realize that we are never alone. The great sheltering wings of God are above us. And we learn how to fly on in faith, growing ever stronger in his love and grace.

And so does the whole Church, the people of God, grow strong in witness of the faith and the power of the Risen Lord.

And He's Off

Text: Acts 13

One of the most dramatic moments in all history seems to be quietly dropped into the text by Luke: the conversion of Saul of Tarsus in chapter nine. A fiery persecutor is knocked off his horse and turned into a fiery evangelist.

It is almost too much. Too much for us, so Luke lets it sit for a while. Too much for Paul, so he spends some time in Arabia. Too much for the Jews, so they try to kill him. Too much for the apostles and the young Church, so Paul is sent quietly back to Tarsus. But not too much for the Spirit. Soon enough Barnabas will be moved to seek him out and bring him back to the center of things to challenge even the head of the apostolic college and evoke the first council of the Church.

The Spirit himself speaking to the Church and acting through the Church sends forth this fiery little man. And a Jewish Church, seeming to most to be little more than a sect, struggling with the question of Gentile admission, suddenly becomes a world Church with communities springing up throughout the Greco-Roman empire until we see the chosen messenger being sent to the emperor himself.

Acts, which until now might have been called the Acts of Peter, can now be called the Acts of Paul. It will trace out his missionary journeys and finally his perilous voyage to Rome. You might get a map for yourself and trace Paul's goings and comings—an amazing amount of travel, for those days with their primitive means. The travel alone is enough to excite our admiration, but as we see it punctuated with shipwreck and stoning, beatings and imprisonment—what a man we have here.

Much of the New Testament—one-half of the "books"—are the letters Paul wrote to these churches he is establishing or would visit, to bishops he would ordain, to the disciples he would come to love. Reading these letters as you encounter these churches and these bishops in the course of your journeying with Paul through Acts will make it a richer and more informative adventure.

In chapter sixteen we will meet Timothy to whom Paul wrote two letters. In the same chapter is the mysterious summons to Philippi which results in the establishment of a church he would later write to. Then in the next chapters we see him among the Thessalonians (17), the Corinthians (18) who enjoyed his presence for a good long period, the Ephesians (18), and the Galatians (18). He would return to see these churches more than once just as he would write to some of them more than once.

For the most part he would keep on the move, ever pressing forward, until in the end he would justifiably proclaim: I have run the course. Tirelessly he trained, seeking his unperishable laurels. It was the Spirit who sent him off, and it was in the Spirit that he triumphantly completed his course.

Text: Acts 20:36ff

I have often wished I could sit down with Saint Paul and ask him which of his many adventures was for him the most challenging, the most unnerving.

Which one do you think?

Getting knocked off his horse at Damascus and hearing unseen voices, or being bundled over the city's walls in a basket to escape a death plot? Being caught in the midst of a riot in the Temple courtyard or being spirited out of the city under a guard of four hundred and seventy to forestall a deadly ambush? Standing before a governor in the earliest days of his mission or later before the pro-counsel and appealing to Caesar? Clinging to life for a night and a day in the sea or having a deadly scorpion cling to him? Being pelted with stones, he who witnessed Stephen's stoning, or feeling a quake break open prison gates?

Paul was exceptionally well prepared by Providence for his special life and mission. A strongly pious youth studying at the feet of the most respected Jewish master made him acceptable to the leaders of the early Church. He knew well the tradition and the promises and now their fulfillment. Roman citizenship and the language of the world enabled him to traverse the world and receive a hearing. He knew how to stand up for his rights and to use Roman justice. But one thing he was not prepared for: the day in Lystra when pagan priests brought bulls and garlands and prepared to offer sacrifice to Paul as the god Hermes. I wonder if this might not have been the most disconcerting experience for this humble servant of the one true God. How ironical it must have seemed on the next journey when Paul spoke to the Athenians of the unknown God and they laughed him to scorn. One day a god, the next a fool.

But Paul sought to be all things to all men. He succeeded remarkably well. He captured hearts. Here in his leave-taking from his beloved Ephesians we get full evidence of this: They all wept as they embraced him and kissed him (20:36).

The more we get to know Paul the more we come to love him. He had his faults. He was fully human. He scrapped with the other apostles often enough and even with the Lord. But he loved them all. And how he loved the Master. He was all heart.

Text: Acts 28

This has been an exciting story.

We began with a scared bunch of fishermen who, when they could think of nothing better to do, went back to their fishing. Left apparently definitively by the one who called them to be something more—fishers of men, sent to catch the whole world—they locked themselves in a room and clung to the Master's Mother (certainly the thing to do when all else seems lost).

And now at the end of Acts, every point of the then known world seems to have been fished in. And a big catch is already in hand in the very capital of that world.

How did it happen?

Jesus, the Master, had said something that was very hard to hear: "It is for your good that I go," adding, "Unless I go the Counselor will not come . . . " (Jn 16:7). Jesus went. The Spirit came. He came in power on Pentecost, and the fearful became fearless and a hundred and twenty became thousands. And so it went.

Step by step the Spirit empowered, guided, and worked with them. He completed the Baptist's work (19:6). He enkindled the Jews (4:31). He opened the way to oneness with the Samaritans (8:17) and then with the Gentiles (10:44).

Jesus himself called Paul but it was the Spirit that sent him forth and guided him in his far-flung tour of evangelization.

The early Church was indeed the Church of the Holy Spirit—the Spirit who blows where he wills, who brings a new birth to fullness of life. No wonder it was an exciting time.

And then? It has gone on. Again and again in the course of nearly two thousand years there have been men and women who have opened to the Spirit and the excitement. As missionaries they have baptized peoples and nations. As evangelists they have blown on smoldering ashes and brought forth a renewed flame. As healers they have healed bodies and healed hearts.

The first century had its Paul. Later centuries had their Bernard of Clairvaux, Francis of Assisi, Francis Xavier. Today we have our Mother Teresa. And tomorrow? What about you?

A Letter for You

Text: Romans 1

A friend of mine tells the story of a Philippine high school student reading a mission magazine about the urban church in Chicago. The student is eager to learn English and reads the magazine a few paragraphs a night, struggling to make progress. The city of Chicago is unknown to him; names are unfamiliar. He catches an insight here and there, but for the most part each sentence stands on its own and does little to draw the high school lad into the drama of salvation history in Chicago. My friend goes on to draw the parallel with the way we read Scripture. We get a few paragraphs at a time usually either in church or on our own. We garner an insight or two. But we rarely get caught up in the whole powerful drama of salvation history, even of a particular city or a particular time.

As we begin the letters of Saint Paul to the different churches I would like to suggest something which perhaps you have never done before. I would like to suggest that you take a Sunday afternoon (or some other space of time sufficiently long) and with some of the eagerness you would have (as much as you can muster) in reading a letter from an important friend or pastor, you sit down and read Paul's letters, one at a time, from end to end.

It is long, this letter to the Romans. Perhaps you might like to have a pen and paper at hand to note passages you want to come back to or you might want to jot things in the margins. Or, if you are the type of reader who can easily do it, you might outline the letter roughly as you go along, or list the main thoughts or subjects as they come up. Try to get a sense of what Paul is saying to you as a Christian of the community church of Rome. Get the overall impact.

After you have finished a whole letter, sit with it for a bit. What is Paul's basic attitude toward the community? Do you like the way Paul is speaking to you? Can you identify with the community Paul addresses—a minority within a minority in a paganized society? Is there anything in Paul's letter that clearly doesn't fit today? How much does fit?

We don't live in Rome of the Colosseum and the Arch of Titus, but our society has enough of its stadiums and war monuments, of the distraction of sports (or what have you) and the anxieties of world domination. Within our community it is not a struggle between circumcision and uncircumcision but rather between what they perhaps represented, conservatives and liberals, or mainliners and charismatics, or Sunday Catholics and social activists—you name them. The same community struggles are with us today. The same faith and grace are here, too. And the ultimate solution is also the same.

Having opened yourself to the experience of the whole, during the week read particular passages in the context of the whole—the ones you have marked or jotted down. Let their message enter more deeply into your life.

So as not to interfere with your first overall reading I will not add any other commentaries in the course of this first letter until the end. I would urge the same approach to the other letters, and in the course of the first overall reading ignore the subsequent commentaries if there are any. Get the sense of the whole letter as a letter and then go back and explore the parts more deeply.

The Letter Writer

Text: Romans 16

How was it that when a little man from Tarsus, and a prisoner at that, approached Rome in chains there was a welcoming party from the city to meet him? In the months that drag on into years, while he awaited trial, persons of all ranks flocked to his lodging to have the privilege of speaking with him. No doubt his reputation grew as time went on, but it had preceded him. He was one of the most powerful letter writers of history. Whose letters have been read regularly, publicly and privately, by millions for nearly two thousand years? There are Peter and John, James and Jude, but no one as much as Paul. This powerful letter writer had written ahead to Rome. And he had written his longest, most compact, and most carefully reasoned letter.

If we lost all the other letters of Paul but this, how much would we have lost? Actually quite a bit, for each letter has its own special revelation of this most extraordinary man. But nothing of his central teaching would have been lost.

This letter to the Romans is a surprising treatise, beginning, after the initial greetings, with the revelation of God in creation and the whole sad story of our pathetic response. There is the ongoing tale of God's continued mercy and outreach, our way of response, encouragement and hope, and final glory.

And then there is the long list of greetings, a clear indication of how all roads lead to Rome. So many of those Paul met in the course of his missionary journeys have gotten there before him. We have heard of these people in Acts. We will meet them again in other letters. This coming together at Rome, this coming together in this letter to the Romans, says something about the centrality of this Pauline text. It is worth most careful study.

CORINTHIANS

Sin City

Text: 1 Corinthians 1

This letter is addressed not only to the Corinthians but to "all those everywhere who call on the name of our Lord Jesus Christ" (1:2), to you and to me. But I think it will be those of us who live in cities who will most readily be able to identify with it: big cities—Sin City (as the Corinth of Paul's time was known)—where dwell "the people of this world who are immoral, the greedy and swindlers, or idolaters" (5:10).

Paul loved his Corinthians. He thanked God always for them. They had it all. Had it all? How could he say that with their divisions, their jealousy and quarreling and their lawsuits, and "sexual immorality of the worst sort." They even got drunk and carried on shamefully at the Lord's Supper.

Paul was writing to very ordinary people. Not many of them were "wise by human standards . . . influential . . . of noble birth" (1:26). And Paul came to them as a very ordinary person, without eloquence or superior wisdom. (He was still smarting from his experience in Athens on the Aeropagus where he tried to use a certain eloquence with the philosophers and was laughed to scorn—Acts 16.)

He knew his beloved Corinthians. He knew their weaknesses, that they had come from among the sexually immoral, idolaters, adulterers, male prostitutes, homosexual offenders, thieves, greedy drunkards, slanderers and swindlers (6:9). He was not surprised, though indeed grieved, to find sin and failure among them. But he knew that Christ "the power of God and the wisdom of God" (1:24) was with them. What he had to say sounded like folly to the wise of this world but Paul brought a new wisdom, one that the Spirit who searches all things, even the deep things of God, reveals to us (2:10). Paul knew that God who raised the Lord from the dead will raise us up also (6:14). He knew that in Christ his beloved Corinthians did indeed have everything.

If we do identify with these inhabitants of Sin City, if we know our own sinfulness, weakness, and folly, we, too, need this living and life-giving knowledge, this new wisdom that gives hope. And so, as we come to these letters we want to

54

call upon the Spirit and ask him to reveal to us through the words of his apostle Paul what "no eye has seen, no ear has heard, no mind has conceived, what God has prepared for those who love him" (2:9) so that our faith "might not rest on men's wisdom, but on the power of God" (2:5).

The Answer Man

Text: 1 Corinthians 7ff

"And now for the matters you wrote about"—so begins the seventh chapter. The rest of this letter to the Corinthians is actually a reply to their letters. Naturally enough, the leadership in the new young church wouldn't have all the answers and would turn to Paul who had brought the faith to enlighten them on the questions that arose.

It is a very mixed collection of questions. Some are quite conditioned by the time and place and would seem to have little relevance to our times: circumcision, slavery, food from sacrifices—although there can be some surprises here.

Recently I was invited to dinner in the home of a devout Hindu. They had their shrine room and before the evening meal the head of the house performed the daily puja or ritual offerings. As we sat down to the table he offered each one some of the *prasad* or sacred food that he had just offered to the deity in his shrine. I was grateful for Paul's wise advice in this letter to the Corinthians as to how to regard this food.

Some of Paul's other responses are very obviously practical: the question of virginity or the single life and marriage, the relation of the sexes, the place of women—but they need to be interpreted. This is not always easy. We could wish sometimes that it were possible to send off a letter to Paul today and see how he would respond to the same questions in the light of the social evolution that has taken place.

The most valuable section of these responses is undoubtedly the chapters concerning spiritual gifts. It certainly has its contemporary relevance, but it also offers Paul the opportunity to develop his magnificent doctrine of the mystical Body of Christ. The richness of the analogy here, of how intimately we belong one to the other and depend one upon the other, and above all the overriding importance of love, is well worth pondering. The thirteenth chapter of this letter will ever be one of the most loved passages in the New Testament.

The long list of questons concludes rightly enough with the ultimate question, that of resurrection. (Not quite the last. It wouldn't be a church if it didn't end with the question of a collection!) "If Christ has not been raised, our preaching is useless and so is your faith" (15:14). This is the ultimate question. Paul gives his long list of witnesses. It is impressive. But in the end it is a matter of faith, the faith that grounds all our belief and is the source of our hope and practice. "But thanks be to God! He gives us the victory through our Lord Jesus Christ" (15:57).

There will always be questions. Practices will change. New challenges will arise. But the fundamental reality of the resurrection of our Lord and Savior, Jesus Christ, will always remain. And so, as Paul admonishes his dear Corinthians, "Always give yourselves fully to the work of the Lord, because you know that your labor in the Lord is not in vain." (15:58).

What a Man!

Text: 1 Corinthians 15:10

Paul is not a man one can sum up in a word or two. He is a man of passion. His love runs deep—we see that in this letter to his dear Corinthians whom he loves with almost a mother's fierceness. Yet, also here we see the father's sternness, the master's threats, irony and even mockery. The whole keyboard of the human spirit is his to play.

But it is played responsibly and responsively. He became "all things to all men" (9:22). To the Jews he was a Jew, a man of tradition, drawing lessons from their common heritage. To those under the law, he, too, was under the law, passing on only what he had received. And to those who had been freed by the gospel, he, too, proclaimed his freedom.

He dared to set himself up as a model—"I urge you to imitate me" (4:16); "I wish that all men were as I am" (7:7)—even as he proclaimed himself as "weak . . . dishonored . . . hungry and thirsty . . . in rags . . . brutally treated . . . homeless . . . scum of the earth . . . refuse of the world." For "when we are cursed, we bless;

57

when we are persecuted, we endure it; when we are slandered, we answer kindly" (4:12).

And he did not hesitate to speak with authority, complementing the very teaching of the Lord: the Lord said this—and I say this. We are baffled by his audacity—and his contradictions: "Judge nothing before the appointed time; wait till the Lord comes" (4:5), but in the next chapter: "I have already passed judgment on the one who did this" (5:3). He proclaimed his freedom, but he was most sensitive to those who had not yet found such freedom in the gospel. "Everything is permissible"—but "Nobody should seek his own good, but the good of others" (10:23).

Paul, who knew the depths of human weakness and misery, knew, too, the power of the Spirit. This passionate man dared to live even beyond himself in the passion of the Spirit. In the end it was "not I, but the grace of God that was with me" (15:10).

A Second Letter

Text: 2 Corinthians

Is this a second letter? It is difficult to tell whether there was in fact another letter—that has not been kept for us—that intervened between this letter and the previous one we have just read. Or is that the letter he refers to in chapter two? Indeed, it is not even clear how often Paul has visited this flock at Corinth. The nice neat chronology we might like is not supplied. We can only piece the fragments of information together. But one thing is clear, and that is that there has been an evolution in Paul and in his relationship with this community.

In 1 Corinthians we saw a powerful, audacious Paul who used authority and dared all things in Christ, strengthened and guided by his Spirit. In this second letter we see more the metal of the man of God as he reveals to a flock grown ever closer to him the struggles he has had to overcome. We have read of some of them in Acts: stoning, shipwreck, riots, beatings, and imprisonment. He adds many others here. He goes into details. And he intones litanies: in danger from rivers, in danger from bandits, in danger from my own countrymen, in danger from Gentiles, in danger in the city, in danger in the country, in danger in the sea. But more important, he speaks more personally and reveals something of the inner anguish, perplexity and distress that he has so constantly borne.

It is a lover speaking here: "We have spoken freely to you, Corinthians, and opened wide our hearts to you" (6:11). He has exposed himself in all his weakness so that God's power working in him might shine through all the more clearly, giving glory to God and hope to his dear Corinthians. They, too, have had and will have their own tribulations. He feels he himself has caused them tribulation with his previous letter and visit when he spoke out as a stern father. Now he would be a minister of God's comfort (he uses the word repeatedly in the first lines of his letter). Paul is at times more mother than father, but he is always the lover and always more loving.

The Generous Giver

Text: 2 Corinthians 8

"There he goes again! Always talking about money. Money, money, money! All he ever talks about is money!"

Well, if all the pastor talks about is money, then that is very sad indeed. He certainly can't claim a precedent in Saint Paul for that, for Paul gives us much solid doctrinal and moral teaching. But you do have to admit that the collection pitch does have a solid grounding in the Scriptures. We have seen it at the end of Paul's first letter to the Corinthians and we will find it again and again in his other letters. But perhaps nowhere is it so developed as here in this second letter to his dear Corinthians.

The persuasive argumentation is well developed. He praises them for their previous generosity. Indeed he has used it to good avail as a model for other communities: they have all heard how generous you have been. And now look how generous they have been—you certainly are not going to be outdone by them, are you? He points to their present good fortune and prosperity. Surely they will go on now to be more generous than ever. They don't have to worry about the future. God, a most generous giver, will take care of them.

Classic statements are coined here: "God loves a cheerful giver" (9:7) and

"Whoever sows sparingly will reap sparingly, and whoever sows generously will also reap generously" (9:6).

The shrewd Corinthians might well have responded to Paul: If God is so generous and is sure to take care, why doesn't he just go ahead and take care of the poor? Why trouble us?

God certainly could. But God wants us to. Why? Because he wants us to have the merit and glory of being like him. Indeed we are called to be perfect as our heavenly Father who lets his rain fall freely upon just and unjust alike. He would rather give freely to us so that we can freely dispense to our brothers and sisters. "Freely have you received, freely give." And thus we will give a powerful witness to the gospel: "Men will praise God for the obedience that accompanies your confession of the gospel and Christ, and for your generosity in sharing with them and with everyone else" (9:13). And we will benefit by the good will and prayer of those we have the privilege to supply: "And in their prayers for you their hearts will go out to you, because of the surpassing grace God has given you" (9:14).

How differently Paul sees things. Yes, this is a new wisdom, a wisdom we all need. Well does Paul cry: "Thanks be to God for his indescribable gift!"

Paul: Who He Truly Is

Text: 2 Corinthians 10

It seems almost like a new letter, or something dropped in from somewhere else. Just as in his first letter to the Corinthians, Paul seemed to have concluded his second letter with a long and powerful collection pitch. And then he erupts into this new chapter. Of course, Paul's letters were not divided into chapters when he wrote them. The determination of chapters and verses is the work of later scholars to facilitate study and reading. The early scribes just wrote on and on, on their long scrolls.

But at this point—chapter ten—there is a very distinct shift. An angry, almost querulous tone breaks out. We have here a hurt lover: "I do not love you? God knows I do!" (11:11). He has sacrificed so much for these dear Corinthians. He has wanted so much for them. But others, "false apostles, deceitful workmen," masquerading as "apostles of Christ," have sought to undo all he has accomplished, have sought to displace him and deny him his place as the father of this community. His poor Corinthians are so easily taken in: "In fact, you even put up with anyone who enslaves you, or exploits you or takes advantage of you or pushes himself forward or slaps you in the face" (11:20).

Paul is almost beside himself with anger. He makes a complete fool of himself—and we are the beneficiaries. For in his heated passion he reveals things he might not otherwise ever have done. He forgets his accustomed humility and self-effacement, at least for a moment. In a torrent he pours out his own self-portrait, as it were—how he sees himself. It is a candid picture. He knows who he is and what he has done. He even goes on to speak of what God has done. Who is this man who has been caught up into paradise and has heard "inexpressible things, things that man is not permitted to tell" (12:4)?

Then Paul catches himself. And as it were to counterbalance this excess he reveals other secrets: a hidden thorn in the flesh, bouts with Satan (12:7). Back to himself, he will boast more gladly about his weaknesses, so that Christ's power might rest upon him and be manifested to all.

Even if this second part of Paul's letter is marked with bristling anger and dour warnings, yet it is so evident that it is in the end all an expression of a passionate love—an all-consuming love for Christ and for those whom Christ has given to him. As we glimpse the sublimity and the depths of this man the only word that can possibly sum it all up is "love."

GALATIANS

Text: Galatians 1

Sometimes a relationship comes to a crisis. And the crisis arises not so much out of the issue at hand as from the fact that one of the parties does not see that the issue is paramount. This is what is happening between Paul and the Galatians.

The relationship is strained. Unlike most every other epistle, Paul does not follow his classical greeting with some sort of affirmation and praise of his correspondents (a good way to begin any dialogue) but immediately he expresses his consternation: "I am astonished. . . ." He uses strong language: perversion . . . eternal damnation.

Paul is really trying to shake these people up and get them to see that there is something of paramount importance at issue here.

What is it that the Galatians are missing?

We have seen it already in Acts. It is the issue that made Paul withstand "to his face" Peter, the Christ-appointed leader of the apostolic band. It brought forth the first Council of the Church. It is the fundamental issue of equality. In Christ "there is neither Jew nor Greek, slave nor free, male nor female" (3:28), black nor white, rich nor poor. All are truly one and equal in the love and re-creation of Jesus Christ.

It is part of the Providential preparation of Paul for his great apostolic mission (something he was very aware of: "God, who set me apart from birth and called me by his grace"—1:15) that he was a Jew of the Jews—he knew the tradition and the rabbinical way of teaching (see 4:22ff)—yet a Roman citizen raised in a Gentile city. Even naturally he was prepared for the new universal good news and it was his responsibility to help his brother Jews raised in the parochial defensiveness of a dominated minority to realize that their distinctiveness—gift though it be from God—was not the most important thing. Far more fundamental is our communion in one humanity; far more important is our oneness in Christ Jesus.

A gospel which establishes or sanctions class distinctions "is really no gospel at all"—no *good news*. It is a blight on humanity, the effect of sin, the product of

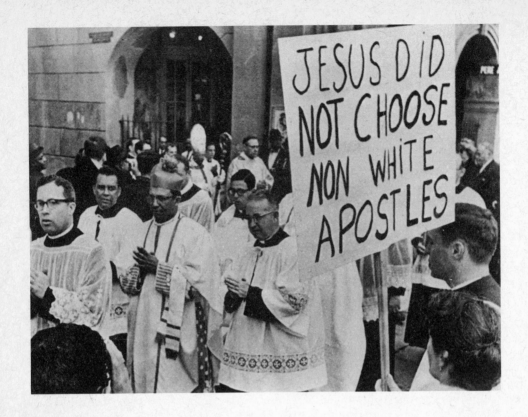

the pride of Babel. And it is still so with us. Indeed if we listen deeply, most of us will find it still lurking in the corners of our own hearts, if it is not even more blatantly present in us. Do we really accept as truly equal with us, one with us in the love of Christ, all men and *women* (Listen, men!), the really poor, those of different skin color, our Jewish sisters and brothers, pagans and tribals, homosexuals and heterosexuals? Christ *did* die for all. All are called to be one in him. All are called to accept oneness in him.

The question here of circumcision and uncircumcision may seem to us minor, passe, something of a particular time and place. But within it resides the denial of the fundamental good news.

No wonder Paul is worked up!

Paul may seem, nonetheless, oversensitive. He takes the Galatians' meandering in doctrine as a personal attack. But perhaps he is not wholly wrong in making it a personal matter. For his credentials as an apostle are important for establishing the truth. He was "an apostle—sent not from men nor by men, but by Jesus Christ and God the Father" (1:1): "I want you to know, brothers [and sisters], that the gospel I preached is not something that man made up. I did not receive it from any man, nor was I taught it; rather, I received it by revelation from Jesus Christ" (1:11).

What Paul teaches here is pure gospel. We have not fully accepted the good news so long as we look upon any human person as inferior or in any way a second class citizen in the kingdom of heaven or the Church on earth.

The Master Race

Text: Galatians 2:21

The ground trembled under the steady, proud march of thousands of feet as the deadly phalanx goose-stepped down the Burgenstrasse. In 1933 it was a moment of high exhilaration for a people. They were proclaimed pure Aryans. Their deeds had but to match their blood and their destiny would be accomplished.

It is a sad fact of history that a world did not tremble in terror and rise up in revulsion when the Burgenstrasse trembled under the pound of those proud feet. Too taken up with present concerns, grasping for momentary well-being, civilized peoples let the deadly phalanx march on until it herded millions of people into incinerators because of their race, or their religious convictions, or their sexual orientation, or other differences. Difference could not be tolerated.

Why is racism, segregation, or any kind of caste system so pernicious?

Because ultimately it proclaims that there is about some people something that makes them better than others—a something that is less than the total gratuity of God. In other words, it makes something human, something created, something we do or are of ourselves the ultimate good. It makes righteousness something we earn or deserve of ourselves. God is no longer God, the ultimate and absolutely gratuitous source of all goodness. In a word, we have created an idol—and usually that idol is ourselves.

Nazism unfortunately is not something totally of the past. We read frequently of neo-Nazis—though in America they are more apt to identify the "master race" as white Anglo-Saxon Catholic or Protestant. The Klan rides again and crosses burn. So innate is the idolatry born of pride.

Paul would have none of it. He knew that even the very law of God himself could be made an idol or rather could be used to make an idol of oneself, a super-human, better than others because a law-keeper. "If righteousness could be gained through the law—or anything else—Christ died for nothing" (2:21).

The Prison of the Law

Text: Galatians 5:1

Have you ever read the Torah, the first five books of the Bible, and counted up all the precepts there? The Jews say there are as many laws as their are bones in the human body. And every one of them has to be religiously observed. No wonder Paul speaks of the bondage of the Law. Just try to imagine what your life would be like if you had to observe carefully every one of those precepts. You would never have a moment of freedom. You would be like a person in prison whose every moment is monitored. "Before this faith came, we were held prisoners by the law, locked up until faith should be revealed" (3:23).

But think how you would be tempted to feel if you were one of the few who was actually freely keeping all these laws. It would be almost impossible not to look down one's nose at the rest of the human herd. Such self-centered right-eousness, created not by a word but at such cost, could hardly escape from a sense of superiority.

Paul knew it from experience: "I was advancing in Judaism beyond many Jews of my own age and was extremely zealous for the traditions of my fathers" (1:14). It was precisely because Paul knew it in his own guts, and knew its per-niciousness—it had turned him into a persecutor—that he realized so deeply what it meant to be baptized into the freedom of Jesus Christ. "It is for freedom that Christ has set us free" (5:1). And Paul tells us what is the inner source of this freedom: "God sent the Spirit of his Son into our hearts, the Spirit who calls out, 'Abba, Father.' So you are no longer a slave, but a son . . . an heir" (4:6).

Text: Galatians 6:15

It is autumn—the time of fruitfulness. As I look out my window I see the orchards. The boughs of the trees hang heavy in the gusty breeze. I remember when we first planted those trees, tender saplings. We watched them through many winters and summers, knowing always that their life could be prematurely cut off. But they have reached maturity. And now red apples and golden pears stand out against the shimmering green leaves. The summer has been long, sometimes hot, sometimes wet. There have been storms. The fruit has been threatened. Some has fallen and is rotting on the ground. Freedom to go its own way has been disastrous.

In the last chapters of this letter life is the current that flows through the text. And from life, a fullness of life, comes fruit. Unfortunately there is more than one kind of life and more than one kind of fruit. Paul details the fruits of sinful nature: "sexual immorality, impurity and debauchery, idolatry and witchcraft, hatred, discord, jealousy, fits of rage, selfish ambition, dissensions, factions and envy, drunkenness, orgies, and the like" (5:19). With more joy and enthusiasm he speaks of the fruits of the Spirit: "love, joy, peace, patience, kindness, goodness, faithfulness, gentleness and self-control" (5:22).

Paul's powerful declaration of freedom is not a license for license. It is rather a freedom to "live by the Spirit"—the Spirit who is love. "You, my brothers [and sisters], were called to be free. But do not use your freedom to indulge the sinful nature; rather serve one another in love" (5:13), so that we may bear the fruits of the Spirit.

In the last letter Paul spoke of sowing and reaping in regard to material goods. Now he speaks of spiritual sowing and reaping: "The one who sows to please the Spirit, from the Spirit will reap eternal life" (6:8).

It is a question of life, and more than life. It is a question of "a new creation" (6:15).

EPHESIANS

_____ **Affirmation**

Text: Ephesians 1

As the Lord Jesus hung on the cross, with all the filial love of a perfect son and with that spousal love he had for the Church, he entrusted his beloved Mother to the Beloved Disciple—and the Disciple and all his disciples to his Mother.

Tradition tells us that Saint John not only took responsibility for Mary, but that he kept her ever close to him, and that they eventually went to Ephesus. Whether their journeying thither was before or after his letter we can hardly say. If it were before, their stabilizing and sanctifying presence might well account for the single blessedness of this community. On the other hand, it might have been the graced picture that comes to us through this letter that attracted John to bring Mary there. We do not know.

What we do know is that this letter to the Ephesians is remarkable among Paul's epistles. There is not a single negative word. The account of Paul's ministry in Ephesus found in Acts (chapter 19) in a way prepares us for this. He spent an even longer period here than in Corinth—over two years. Right from the start he had a good reception. Just as John the Baptizer prepared the way for Jesus, so John's disciples had prepared the way here for Jesus' disciple. Ephesus quickly became a center for the proclamation of the faith to all of Asia Minor. Even when the jealous managed to spark a riot against Paul and his teaching in Ephesus, it added up to nothing. It was peacefully dispersed by a calming word. Ephesus and the Ephesians were special.

Paul's letter to them then is something special. It is a letter of affirmation. It is a celebration, a proclamation of the glory of being Christian. Basically Paul says: By God's great mercy you are a Christian—live it, glory in it, be grateful. What God has done in Christ he will do in us; in fact, he has already done it: "God raised us up with Christ and seated us with him in the heavenly realms in Christ Jesus" (2:6). (Though some days it sure doesn't feel that way!)

There is near our abbey a center called the House of Affirmation. It is in fact the center of a whole international network of such houses. In the ministry of

68

these houses there is employed theology along with psychological sciences. Rather than centering exclusively on the patient's ills, this House of Affirmation underlines each person's reality as seen in its fullness through theology. It doesn't deny weaknesses. Paul here readily acknowledges the sinful past of these Ephesians (2:1); indeed he identifies with it (2:3). But he issues a powerful call and gives powerful support for living out of one's fullness. This is affirmation: seeing the true goodness of the person and, in affirming that, giving them the conscious possession of the forces that lie within them to be great in Christ Jesus. It is not the glorification of the created person in himself or herself. In the end all glory is to God, the source of all of this goodness: "For we are God's workmanship, created in Christ Jesus to do good works, which God prepared in advance for us to do" (2:10).

Borne up by the exhilaration of the great reality which he affirms (the affirmer himself is always powerfully affirmed when he affirms others) Paul lets pour forth from his soul one of the most beautiful prayers in all literature:

For this reason I kneel before the Father, from whom his whole family in heaven and on earth derives its name. I pray that out of his glorious riches he may strengthen you with power through his Spirit in your inner being, so that Christ may dwell in your hearts through faith. And I pray that you, being rooted and established in love, may have power, together with all the saints, to grasp how wide and long and high and deep is the love of Christ, and to know this love that surpasses knowledge—that you may be filled to the measure of all the fullness of God. Now to him who is able to do immeasurably more than all we ask or imagine, according to his power that is at work within us, to him be glory in the church and in Christ Jesus throughout all generations, for ever and ever! Amen.

Times Change

Text: Ephesians 5

Paul had nothing to complain about with his Ephesians. Yet, the practical Paul is always with us. Difficulties could arise. Haven't they everywhere else? So he takes the opportunity in this letter of affirmation to add a bit of exhortation and explanation.

Communities had been splintered by differences. So Paul seeks to explain, using one of his favorite images, that in this Body of Christ, the community, there are different roles to be fulfilled—just as in the human body. This is necessary "so that the Body of Christ may be built up" (4:12). Each has his or her own unique gift from the Lord. Each is to show forth some facet of the overwhelming beauty of Christ.

The letter is filled with exhortation, not just to good morals but to praise and thanksgiving. And Paul constantly breaks out into praise himself. His moral teaching is very practical, though we might have some difficulties with it today. The sexist attitude in assigning roles to men and women (5:22ff), and the acceptance of slavery (6:5ff), are a product of the times. These are magnificently theologized by Paul. A Christian slave obeying his master can see Christ in him and be obeying Christ when he obeys and serves his master. And a wife can and should see Christ in her husband. But Paul's rich theology, which sees the relationship between wife and husband and husband and wife in marriage as a sacrament of the relation of the Church to Christ and Christ to the Church, can certainly still stand with the roles of wife and husband reversed. For indeed, as Paul has said, in Christ there is neither male nor female. It is the loving, caring, self-sacrificing and bonded relationship between two persons that is sacramental.

Times change. Society evolves. But the grace of Christ ever continues to work within. It is not bound up with one set of social mores. Christ belongs to all the times and all the ages. And his grace sanctifies them all.

PHILIPPIANS

Prison Letters

Text: Philippians 1

Last year one of my friends was sentenced to a year in jail for the part he played in a witness against the production and deployment of nuclear weapons. I wrote to the judge who sentenced him, thanking him for giving Art this time of repose during which, without concern for securing his livelihood—guest of the state that he was—he could give himself to prayer, reflection, and writing, preparing himself for the important work that lay ahead of him as a dedicated peacemaker.

When we think of prison letters we think immediately of Bonhoeffer and of Father Alfred Delp. Actually, at least four of the dozen or so letters we have from the pen of Saint Paul are prison letters. The enforced solitude and quiet that one sometimes finds behind prison bars affords men of the Spirit an opportunity to listen to God more deeply. And the fruit of that listening is sometimes shared. It is apt to be the deepest and most beautiful fruit coming from the pen of a writer. In the space that imprisonment provides he is more apt to touch, not the nagging questions that have plagued his everyday ministry, but the deep underlying realities—the sources of true meaning and joy in his life.

As Paul wrote to the Philippians there no doubt came to his mind his first visit to that city and his prison experience there, one of his first (Acts 16). This is perhaps another reason why this letter is so filled with joy. Prison bars and gates, as he so well experienced there, are no match for the Spirit of God who is the Spirit of joy. Don't you think Paul was human enough to smile a bit as the magistrates came cowering and escorted him out of prison?

Text: Philippians 1:23

"I am torn between the two: I desire to depart and be with Christ, which is better by far; but it is more necessary for you that I remain in the body" (1:23).

For Paul it is not really a question of being and not being. It is rather a question of being there or being here. And it is a question of joy: to have his own personal joy complete there or to have his joy multiplied by bringing joy to others here.

We are not here talking about the passing emotion of joy, usually all too quickly passing—a wonderful thing to have, but so elusive. No, we are talking about true, deep joy—the kind of joy that comes from seeing those we love happy, growing, finding fulfillment. "I will continue with all of you for your progress and joy in the faith, so that through my being with you again your joy in Christ Jesus will overflow on account of me" (1:25f), the joy that comes from knowing the meaning of our lives and seeing that fulfilled. "Forgetting what is behind and straining toward what is ahead, I press on toward the goal to win the prize for which God has called me heavenward in Christ Jesus" (3:13f).

What is happiness? There are many definitions abroad. Charlie Brown has his own wonderful collection. And I am sure you have yours. But here is mine. Try it on for size: Happiness consists in knowing what you want and in knowing you have it or are on the way to getting it.

Most people are unhappy because they do not know what they want—they don't know the real wants of their humanity and their divinity, that participated divinity they have received in baptism. They are constantly frustrating themselves. And where they have to make a choice, they don't want to, because every choice means giving up something. (Getting married means giving up every other girl in the world—yet what groom goes to the altar thinking about the girls he is giving up?) But we can be happy only when we find something or Someone big enough for us and are ready to put our whole being on the line for it.

Paul knew what he wanted, where he was going, and how to get there. And he was on the way. And he was happy. This letter is filled with joy. Ultimately our joy comes from Christ and is one with his. As Paul proclaims this he gives us the gift of one of the oldest Christian hymns we have (2:5). In his abounding joy he cries out to us: "Rejoice in the Lord always. I will say it again: Rejoice!" (4:4).

From the Least Comes the Most

Text: Philippians 4:14

In many ways this rather brief letter to the Philippians is similar to the previous one to the Ephesians. Paul is not particularly preoccupied with any great problems, though the Philippians obviously have had them with the Judaizers (3:2). And there have been divisions or a tendency toward them (4:2). The letter we have here is more of a personal note, a thank you note. There is some exhortation, as before. But, again, things seem to be going along fairly well.

In some ways what is happening at Philippi is more wonderful. Paul had had much less time to plant the Church there. And what strange elements he had to begin with: an Asiatic cloth merchant, a slave girl who told fortunes, a rather hysterical prison guard. He himself was imprisoned and soon sent on his way.

Yet Paul had a special bonding with these Philippians. He accepted from them what he would not accept from most of his converts and their communities. He allowed them to provide for his own personal needs. He trusted them not to use this against him.

It is often the poor, the outcast, the marginal who know how to care for others and from their little share whatever they can, leaving their benefactor feeling free from debt.

COLOSSIANS

Text: Colossians 1

There is something about this letter that is different from any of the other letters we have so far read. It is addressed to a community which Paul himself has not founded or personally ministered to. He has not met these Christians of Colossae, yet they are dear to him and he in some way considers them his. For was he not sent to be the apostle of the Gentiles, all the Gentiles?

Yet in most ways this letter is very much the same as some of the foregoing. The standard format: greetings, prayer, doctrine, practical applications, and closing personal tidbits. The content, too. It especially resembles the letter to the Ephesians, another community "orderly and firm in faith" (2:5). It is as though, like a modern evangelist, Paul used a word processor to send out virtually the same letter to various groups of adherents. Paul was in prison. He had no word processor. But these basic ideas were lodged in his mind and there was relatively little in the way of new stimuli coming in. It is no wonder there is a great likeness in what was coming out.

Yet there is in each letter he writes some proper element not found in any of the others, or not underlined in quite the same way. He is aware of it and urges these Colossians to share their letter with the Laodiceans and in turn to share their letter—a letter we do not have today.

In this letter there is the usual warning against the Judaizers. But there is in addition a concern about the mystery cults and especially any syncretism. Christianity, with its God who really became a man like us and spoke to us in very direct human language, can seem too simple, too earthy, not sufficiently spiritual.

But Paul makes no bones about it. His statement is clear and strong: "In Christ all the fullness of the Deity lives in bodily form" (2:9). You cannot find any more of God, or of the Transcendent, or of the Spirit than you can find in Jesus Christ. It is all there.

Those other cults may have "an appearance of wisdom, with their self-imposed worship, their false humility and their harsh treatment of the body" (2:23),

75

but it is a false wisdom. The fullness of Wisdom lies in Christ and in the teaching of his apostles and disciples in his Church.

Paul also emphasizes here the importance of integration into the living body of Christ, which is the Church. He becomes very graphic in his use of his favorite imagery: "the whole body, supported and held together by its ligaments and sinews" (2:19).

The desire for a supportive community in belief and practice on the spiritual journey is a very deep one and a connatural one. Undoubtedly one of the reasons why some Christians are drawn to the cults is because they promise this kind of supportive community and such is not readily experienced in large parish communities, communities of the lukewarm. But in fact the church does offer something much more substantial—a profound unity in the Body of Christ. If only we would live that unity, what community we would have, for it is a community that reaches to the very heavens and will exist forever.

No wonder Paul cries: "Since you have been raised with Christ, set your hearts on things above, where Christ is seated at the right hand of God. Set your minds on things above, not on earthly things" (3:1f).

THESSALONIANS

What a Preacher!

Text: 1 Thessalonians

This first letter to the Thessalonians is reputed to be one of Paul's earliest. He was back from his first missionary voyage into what we know today as Europe. The journey was fresh in his mind, every detail of it. He remembered well the riot at Thessalonica (Acts 17), one of his first but certainly not his last. Perhaps the most painful part of the memory of this particular riot was the fact that it was others, not himself, who suffered in it. For once he got away safe.

What a powerful preacher of the Word Paul must have been. He enters a city as a stranger, unknown to all, penniless. And soon the whole city is stirred up and everybody is shouting his name—pro or con.

That is the power of the Word and of a man who is of the Word. No flattery, no masks. Clear witness—cost what it may. No personal gain. Indeed Paul boasts here that the days of preaching were followed by nights of labor for self-support, even while he maintains that the preacher does have the right to be supported by those to whom he ministers.

We see here that the young Paul was not all that sure of himself, or should we say, of his God. He tells how soon after sowing the seed in Thessalonica he sent Timothy back to check things out. A surer, more mature apostle would come to see that one sows, another waters, while God gives the increase when and how he knows best. That's enough.

As he writes this letter, though, Paul is quite sure of his Thessalonians. His letter is a simple one of love, affirmation, and encouragement.

Text: 2 Thessalonians 1

We speak of the epistles of Saint Paul. That is not quite accurate. In most of the cases the letter is from Paul and one or more of his co-workers, most often Timothy. Look back over the letters we have read and see how often this is true.

Paul believed in walking and working with others. Even the bad experience he had with Barnabas in his earliest days (Acts 15:39) did not disillusion him. We will suffer at times from those whom we have chosen to walk with us. Jesus did: "One who has dipped his hand into the bowl with me will betray me." Yet, as God said: It is not good for man to be alone.

But we don't have just a message from Paul, Silas and Timothy (or whoever it might be in a particular letter). We have grace and peace and the source of all that is continued in the letter coming from God the Father and the Lord Jesus Christ. God is part of the team. That is why Paul's letters are so powerful.

Whenever we talk or work with others a new power comes into play: "Where two or three are together in my name, there am I in the midst of them."

The presence and the power of God is always available to us.

But the team does not show up only in the senders. Most of Paul's letters end with a whole litany of greetings. The co-workers surrounding him send greetings. The co-workers at the other end receive them. Again, go back and look over the letters we have already seen and note how many of these there are, and what a variety. In the letter to the Colossians there are greetings from six and greetings to innumerable others, besides the two messengers being sent.

Yes, there are the messengers. In days when letters were much more cumbersome things to write and to deliver, and confidentiality of the written word was most difficult to achieve, the messenger often had the more important role. It was his to fill out the message: "Tychius, the dear brother and faithful servant in the Lord, will tell you everything, so that you also may know how I am and what I am doing. I am sending him to you for this very purpose, that you may know how we are, and that he may encourage you" (Eph 6:21). If there was something really confidential to be conveyed it would be the messenger who would convey it viva voce. The trusted bearer of a letter came with a certain power and authority. This was understood.

In the end, as must be the case for anyone who is going to minister successfully in Christ's name, Paul's message comes from the Church, the members of the Body together with their Head collaborating together for the upbuilding of the whole Body.

He's Coming! When?

Text: 2 Thessalonians 2

When is he coming? "Like a thief in the night" (1 Thes 5:2). Those living in the light need have no fear.

In his previous letter to the Thessalonians Paul gave only a bit of doctrinal teaching in what was otherwise a paternal letter of encouragement. The flock in Thessalonica was evidently most receptive. They were born (so to speak) out of a relatively short apostolic visit, one that was abruptly ended (Acts 17). They heard the Word and took it to heart. They were a house built on rock.

Now they seem to have taken Paul's brief doctrinal note a bit too seriously— at least some of them.

Paul quiets them, warns them against false rumors and prophets of doom. He explains more fully what might be expected before the coming of the Lord.

He also turns to those who have, it seems, taken his teaching as an opportunity to indulge their sloth. The end is near—so why work?

Paul's response? Get to work. Support yourself. Contribute to others. Right to the end.

Paul held labor in high esteem. Repeatedly in his letters he boasts of supporting himself. Without hesitation he can point to himself as an example. His ministry was indeed labor and deserved recompense. Yet over and above this he earned by the work of his hands.

This close identification with the poor and laboring is a word the successors of the apostles, priests and bishops, might well need to hear today—all of us who are called to the ministry. Perhaps it points to part of the reason why our preaching doesn't start riots and transform cities. We are so little threat to anyone. So few of us can say to the poor, to the workers to whom we are supposed to be ministering: Be imitators of me. Those who can—praise and thank God for them—stand out like Paul, the shining lights of our Church today.

LETTERS OF TIMOTHY

A Church Emerges

Text: 1 Timothy 1

There is a lot of fight still in Paul. There always will be, for he is fired by the Spirit. Age won't take its toll. But he is in prison. And Nero is making sport of Christians in the most inhuman ways imaginable. Paul's time may be short. He has fought the good fight. He has run the course. He has built up a worldwide Church. A structure is emerging.

For most of his missionary years Timothy has been at his side—his "auxiliary bishop," we might say, certainly his trouble-shooter. But Paul's travels are over. And Timothy has now been sent to head one segment of the church Paul has helped to establish, the church of Asia Minor, with its center at Ephesus.

To Timothy will fall the responsibility of constituting the "overseers"—the bishops of the other cities of the area. He will have to ordain deacons, too, to assist him in the care of his own city and its surroundings. Paul hasn't thrown in the towel yet. He may yet get there himself, and he would like to. But just to be sure, he is writing to give Timothy guidelines in choosing the men who are to serve the people of God in leadership roles.

While married bishops have passed from the scene in the Catholic Church, married deacons are re-emerging. In any case, the qualities have not changed. Those called to ministry can well use Paul's third chapter here as a good point of departure for reflection on the quality of life they bring to their service.

We find mention here of two other groups who found their place in the early structure of the Church: widows and elders. These, too, may again emerge as structured groups in the ongoing renewal. We can identify their presence already in some ways in the altar societies, the ladies' guilds, the ushers, and other such groups who serve so faithfully and well in any functioning parish. When the Second Vatican Council spoke of the development of new ministries in the Church, it certainly meant to include the possibility of the re-emergence of old ones which might find meaning again as the more recent congregations of religious diminish,

priests grow fewer in number, and the local lay community takes more and more responsibility for the local church.

Bishops might ponder Paul's first letter to Timothy for more reasons than one. And so might we all.

As a Son with His Father

Text: 1 Timothy 3:14

Timothy had indeed been "as a son with his father." The last four letters have opened with greetings from Paul and Timothy. For years they had traveled to-

83

gether. If at times Timothy was sent out on missions on his own, it was as Paul's vicegerent, soon to return to his side. Now Timothy had come into his own. And his "father" has a word of fatherly advice for him.

Paul does write this letter for the benefit of the church. There is very important instruction in it in regarding the constitution of the hierarchy. There is concern about syncretism, the inroads of "superior" ideas from the mystery cults. Lesser matters are treated, such as the prayer of the faithful and the conduct of women in church. Some of this still needs to be heard, and some of it is relevant to the social order of the time, like the advice to slaves.

But in this letter we would not be mistaken if we saw as the overriding concern of Paul the personal guidance and advice he gives to Timothy himself. Here, too, there is a distinction to be made.

Some of the advice is made in the context of Timothy's official role as head of the church of Ephesus. There is a time to command with authority, even the rich. And there is a time for great gentleness and respect.

And then there is very personal advice for this son of his spirit—for his own spiritual growth, and for his physical well being: "Stop drinking only water, and use a little wine because of your stomach and your frequent illnesses" (5:22). Paul makes an appeal for a healthy and freeing simplicity: "Godliness with contentment is a great gain. For we brought nothing into the world, and we can take nothing out of it. But if we have food and clothing we will be content with that" (6:6).

How often in the later years Timothy must have taken this letter out and with tears gently rolling down his cheeks read again the wise advice that said so much. What a gift from God to have had such a spiritual father.

It certainly is a great gift from God to have someone walk closely with us on the spiritual path and to surround us with such love and counsel. A great spiritual father once said to me: "You know the difference between a natural father and a spiritual father? In natural paternity it is the father who decides to become a father. In spiritual paternity it is the son who calls forth the spiritual father to nurture him." Perhaps one of the elements that could be most life-giving in the renewal of Christian life would be the re-emergence of the role of the spiritual father. We are missing something, missing very much, an immense support on our spiritual journey, if we do not call forth someone to nuture us as a spiritual father or mother as we grow in the life of the Lord.

Text: 2 Timothy

Back in my college days I used to visit the wards of the County Hospital each week with the members of the Legion of Mary. I came to know and love those dear old folks, many of whom had no one this side of the grave—at least no one who remembered them or cared. I remember especially Dottie, a gentle, rather melancholy old women in her eighties. She always seemed to wait for my coming. She listened to the Scriptures, and prayed quietly with me, her eyes glistening with tears. She said little but always her busy fingers were clutching at some little thing—her shawl, some letters, a bit of ribbon or paper. Everything was passing, disappearing. There was just this little bit to hang on to.

We see very definite signs of aging in Paul in this second letter to his beloved son. He wants now his cloak, his scrolls, some bits of parchment. He moans of the "terrible times" that are coming. Everyone is abandoning him: Demas, Crescens, Titus. He begs his beloved Timothy: "Do your best to come to me quickly" (4:9). For who else will take care of him? In his previous letter he wrote about the responsibility of children to care for aging parents and grandparents (1 Tim 5:3ff). He wrote with inner feeling, but now the feelings are acutely his own.

This second letter to Timothy is yet more personal, tender: Remember when you were a little boy. He speaks of Timothy's mother and grandmother. It is now evident to Paul that he is never going to get to Ephesus. Maybe that is why there is so much in this book about suffering: "I am suffering even to the point of being chained like a criminal" (2:9).

The paternal instinct is very evident here, the desire to go on living in some way in one's offspring. Emotion is high. Timothy knows him, knows his mission, knows what he has accomplished. Now Timothy must go on and do likewise—be a chip off the old block, if I might use such a profane phrase in a context so ladened with human feeling. As Paul urges Timothy on, he reaches out in all directions for images: soldiery, athletics, farming, housekeeping. In the end he realizes that nothing carries the fullness of the message he wants to convey: "Reflect on what I am saying, for the Lord will give you insight into all this" (2:7)

But the old fire is not yet gone out of Paul. He can go on to write: "In the presence of God and of Christ Jesus, who will judge the living and the dead, and in view of his appearing and his kingdom, I give you this charge" (4:1). There is no diminishment here!

I cannot leave these letters to Timothy without noting that gift Paul gives us in them of two more of the early Christian hymns, so rich in theological content. Faith flows out of worship even as it grounds it.

LETTER OF TITUS

=== **Crete**

Text: Titus

It is still the old man in prison writing. He is alone in his greeting and for the first time heaps up descriptions of himself as if trying to assure his existence and worth. Unlike the letters to Timothy this is not a personal, warm-hearted letter. It is more a thing of business.

Titus' position is different, too. He is not so much an archbishop, as Timothy is in the chosen see of Ephesus, but a legate *a latere,* one who has gone forth from the side of Paul to care for the church of Crete in his name.

Again there is the same concern about the constitution of good bishops—here called elders. For them we find the same litany of virtues as we find in the letter to Timothy. It is well worth pondering.

As one reads, one gets the impression that Paul did not think very highly of the Cretans. In this he is a product of his times: "Cretans are always liars, evil brutes, lazy gluttons"—so one of their own. Nor does he seem to have sent one of his best men there. He gives Titus a very basic primer for preaching, what to say to old men, old women, young men, slaves, etc. "These then are the things you should teach" (2:15). To undergird this he reminds the hapless Titus of the legate's unimpressive beginnings, though Paul is gallant enough and humble enough to identify with these, confessing them as his own: "At one time we too were foolish, disobedient, deceived and enslaved by all kinds of passions and pleasures. We lived in malice and envy, being hated and hating one another" (3:3f).

This letter is almost one of unrelieved drabness. There are a few rich theological sentences, but no phrase of this epistle has become a classic.

LETTER OF PHILEMON

An Offer You Can't Refuse

Text: Philemon

Talk about putting pressure on! When Paul wants something, he wants it—and usually gets it, too.

And Paul wanted something from Philemon—something of significance. Philemon is a Christian now, but he still is a somebody in the secular world. He has been humiliated. And Paul is asking him to swallow this and to do good to the one who has caused his humiliation—a slave.

And so he goes to work:

First, he asks this of Philemon publicly, before all the Church. It is difficult to say "no" in front of a crowd, especially a crowd that looks up to you and respects you.

He then lays on the recital of Philemon's known goodness, his faith and love, his generosity: "You will do even more than I ask" (21). Paul claims the right to demand this of Philemon, but he will forego his right and pull on the strings of love. He expresses his own sacrifice for Philemon in sending Onesimus back to him. If Philemon has been humiliated by the run-away, still he has really gained by the whole experience, or will.

Paul then goes on to identify himself with Onesimus. And from this position he claims his personal relationship with his dear Philemon: "You owe me your very self" (29).

He even talks of coming soon to Philemon's house—this prisoner who is in fact going nowhere but to a martyr's death.

If it were anyone else, all of this would be suspect, indeed. But knowing the passionate Paul we can believe it is in fact all love. He is truly seeking what he sees to be best for all. Philemon will grow even as Onesimus finds freedom.

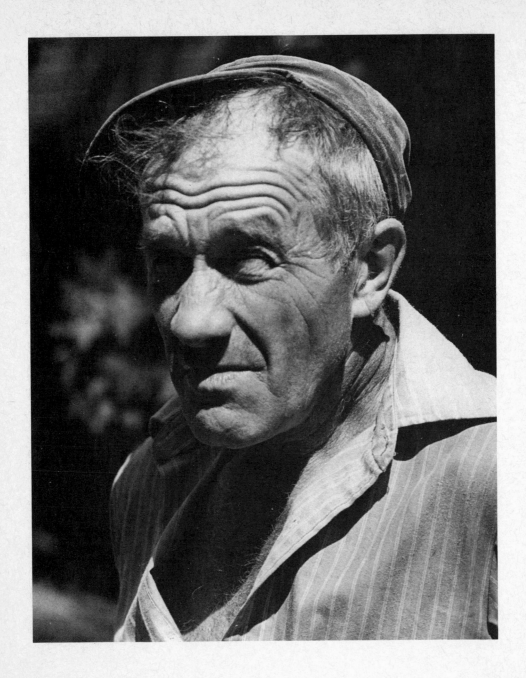

90

HEBREWS

Continuation

Text: Hebrews 1

We do not know who is the author of this letter to the Hebrews. At one time it was thought to be Paul but that is evidently not the case. I do not know if anyone has ever conjectured that it might be Matthew or the man who did the Greek redaction of the first gospel. It certainly can be seen as a continuation of the Gospel of Matthew. There Jesus is shown to be the fulfillment of the prophecies in his human life, his passion and death: Ought not the Christ to have suffered these things and so fulfilled the Scriptures? Now we are shown how the glorification of Christ is also the fulfillment and completion of the Old Testament. Matthew cited the sacred text with great frequency, but this author does so much more. Make a collage of the texts he quotes or refers to and see what an image of Christ you have.

Comparisons are odious—but not for our author. He is intent upon demonstrating to his readers the superiority of the new covenant. Its Founder is "worthy of greater honor than Moses" (3:3). He offers better hope (7:18), a better covenant (7:22), better promises (8:6). His is a greater priesthood (7:6) with a superior ministry (8:6) celebrated in a greater and more perfect tabernacle (9:11).

The author of this letter to the Hebrews has gone far beyond the Old Testament in his theology, but not in his spirituality. It is still that of the slave or servant, filled with fear, threats and promises of rewards. When he does speak of sonship it is only to present the Father as a strict disciplinarian (12:7ff). We are alienated sinners far from God, outside the holy of holies. We need a mediator to commune with him. Love hardly seems to be a word in this author's vocabulary. With his rabbinical scholarship he has given us a finely wrought thesis but there is no warmth in it. Certainly there is nothing of Paul's passionate love for Christ or our oneness and intimacy with him.

We Do Have a Priest

Text: Hebrews 8:1

Undoubtedly, if we have been truly listening as we have moved along through this New Testament we have learned this: "The word of God is living and active. Sharper than any double-edged sword, it penetrates even to dividing soul and spirit, joints and marrow; it judges the thoughts and attitudes of the heart. Everything is uncovered and laid bare before the eyes of him to whom we must give an account" (4:12f). The deep wounds of our sin have been laid bare. We need a priest.

And we do have a priest, a priest who "meets our need—one who is holy, blameless, pure, set apart from sinners, exalted above heavens" (7:26), yet like us in all things but sin. To fully understand priesthood, and in particular the priesthood of Christ, we need to study the Old Testament and the divinely constituted priesthood we find there. Indeed, an understanding of the prophecies, types, and figures of the Old Testament is necessary to fully appreciate Jesus and the role he is meant to play in our lives.

In the best rabbinical fashion over the course of several chapters our author carefully brings forward text after text, type after type, and, weaving them all together with the new revelation, gives us the full image of Christ, our High Priest.

Having such a priest "let us draw near to God with a sincere heart in full assurance of faith" (10:22).

Faith

Text: Hebrews 11:1

"Faith is being sure of what we hope for and certain of what we do not see" (11:1).

How can you or I be certain of what we do not see, be sure of what we hope for? We can because someone trustworthy has told us.

Every day we believe things we are told. How else could we function in this world of ours? We believe most people—perhaps too much. We learn that some people are deceivers. Perhaps we have had the sad experience of finding ourselves deceivers. Sometimes, too, we are deceived not because persons wanted to deceive us but because they themselves were deceived.

But God can neither be deceived, nor deceive. He knows everything and he speaks only the truth. When God tells us, we can be certain. And when God promises, we can be sure that that promise will be fulfilled.

The author of this letter to the Hebrews points to the example of the man most important to these people, the father of their race, Abraham. And we must admit there could hardly be a greater example of faith and hope.

Abraham was living evidently a prosperous enough life in his own country when the Lord called him forth with a promise. He was meant for greater things.

Think of the courage it took to set out to an unknown land, the nature of the inhabitants, their language and customs unknown. And then to go on year after year on the promise that this was to be his land and that of his offspring—the faith it took especially when the years rolled by and there were no children—and then to believe that he and his wife, nearing a hundred, would finally have that son and heir. Undoubtedly Isaac's belated birth reinforced Abraham's faith, yet what a challenge there was when God asked him to slay that son. It was more a challenge of loyalty and love. Abraham passed it well, and his race did grow and multiply to give us all at length a savior and a new faith and hope.

What was the key to Abraham's faith—and to that of all the great believers like him? The author gives us the key here: "They were longing for a better country—a heavenly one." They had listened in the depths of their hearts. And they knew there was nothing in this world that could ultimately satisfy them. They turned to God and listened. From him they learned about what they did not see but what would indeed satisfy. And they heard his promise. They believed and followed. And in the end they found.

If we listen only to our own senses and imaginations, feelings and thoughts, we will spend our life chasing after hopes that will always delude, promises that we will never fulfill. But if we listen to our deepest hearts and aspire for the homeland that will fulfill all our deepest longings, like Abraham we will listen to God, "certain of what we do not see" and "sure of what we hope for."

Perfect Joy

Text: James 1

"Brother Giles, in what consists perfect joy? I will tell you." And to the astonished little brother Saint Francis goes on to recount his idea of perfect joy: getting turned away, rebuffed, beaten, and abused.

Francis must have been inspired by the words with which Saint James opens his letter to the Hebrews—the twelve tribes scattered among the nations: "Consider it pure joy, my brothers, whenever you face trials of many kinds" (1:2). Jerusalem, the holy city, with its glorious temple, has been utterly destroyed. The chosen people of God have been scattered to the four winds. Their sufferings have indeed been great. And now James, the servant of the Lord Jesus Christ (and perhaps his "brother," a cousin related by blood—we are not sure who this James is, even if he is one of the two Jameses who were found among the Twelve), brings them good news. Their sufferings will lead them to maturity, completeness, until they lack nothing. And if they do lack anything they have but to ask God and he will give it to them.

We sometimes wonder, though, if this is true. Why are our prayers not answered? Jesus did say: "Ask, and you shall receive." And we ask and we do not receive. James here tells us why: when we ask we must believe and not waver in our hearts. There can be no room for doubt in our prayer if we expect it to be heard.

James is a very practical pastor. His instruction is simple and concise. "Let your 'Yes' be yes, and your 'No,' no. Is any one of you in trouble? He should pray. Is anyone happy? Let him sing songs of praise. Is any one of you sick? He should call the elders of the church to pray over him and anoint him with oil in the name of the Lord" (5:12ff—we have here the origin of the sacrament of the sick). Very practical! "What good is it, my brothers [and sisters], if one claims to have faith but has no deeds?" (2:14). James uses rich and concrete imagery. His instruction on the use of the tongue in chapter three is a classic, as is his looking glass (1:23f).

Some years ago one of Japan's most outstanding Zen masters visited a Trappist monastery. He was profoundly impressed. He had had no idea that such sincere monastic practice existed in the West. He wanted to spend some time with these monks and offered to lead them in a *seshein*— a Zen retreat.

But he wanted it to be a Christian Zen retreat. During his time there he wore the Cistercian habit. He chanted in choir with the monks. In the meditation walks he had them chant *Kyrie eleison*.

The principal part of a Zen retreat, though, is sitting on a cushion in a very attentive posture and meditating on a *koan*—an enigmatic statement—until one makes a breakthrough and perceives the inner reality of the statement. Roshi, the Zen master, searched the New Testament to find Christian *koans*. He could have found some very good ones in James' epistle: "Consider it pure joy whenever you face trials of many kinds" (1:2). "The brother in humble circumstances ought to take pride in his high position" (1:9). "After desire has conceived, it gives birth to sin" (1:15). "Mercy triumphs over judgment" (2:13).

The advice the Zen master gave the monks as they entered into their retreat was very much that of Saint James: "Everyone should be quick to listen, slow to speak and slow to become angry" (1:19). The meditator was to spend hours pondering his *koan*. He was not to rush to the master with the first thought or glimmer of understanding that came into his head—otherwise he might well get hit with the master's little stick or at least verbally lashed. He was to listen and listen, and not get angry.

Christianity, of course, has its own methods, old and new. One of them, the old method of *meditatio*—somewhat different from our modern discursive meditation—is quite similar to Zen meditation. The disciple would receive from his spiritual father or from his *lectio*—listening to Scripture—a "word of life"—a phrase or sentence which he would repeat continuously in his mind and sometimes on his lips, until "the mind descended into the heart," that is, until the deep inner meaning of the phrase formed the heart and caused it to erupt or burn with a prayerful response to God.

There is though a very important difference between any true Christian meditation practice and those of the East. The Christian always knows that he does not know. We do not know how to pray as we ought. "Don't be deceived, my dear brothers [and sisters]. Every good and perfect gift is from above, coming down from the Father of the heavenly lights. . . . He chose to give us birth through the word of truth" (1:16ff).

But the masters, Zen or Christian, would agree on this: meditation must overflow into life. As the Roshi would say: you can best judge one's meditation by the way he sweeps the walk. Or as James says: "Do not merely listen to the word, and so deceive yourselves. Do what it says" (1:22).

And the results? "The man who looks intently into the perfect law that gives freedom, and continues to do this, not forgetting what he has heard, but doing it—he will be blessed in what he does" (1:25). He will find the true freedom of the child of God.

A Wisdom Full of Mercy

Text: James 3:17

The phone rang. It was 11 P.M. Father Jim was new at Saint Mary's. Indeed he was new at the priesthood—only four weeks. The oil was hardly dry on his hands. The call was a shock: an auto crash, with four of "his" young parishioners, head-on. When he reached the emergency room he was ushered into a long darkened room. There were three young corpses. What was a priest to do? Pray? Anoint? Cry? As he came out a policeman pointed to a knot of three agitated adults just at the door. "Father, tell the couple on the right their two kids are dead. And the one on the left—her son is in X-ray. You can take them over there." He pointed to a room opposite.

As Father Jim tried to usher them in, they became more agitated. The man insisted more and more forcefully: "I want to see my kids." By the time the priest got them seated, the father was glaring and barking. Father Jim's head reeled. "Why can't I see my kids?" What could Father say? "Because they are dead." They all burst into tears, Jim included. What a brutal way to tell them.

It was a long night. Father waited for the parents of the third victim, but it was discovered that they were out of town. He offered to drive the other parents home, but they refused. They lived several towns away. Jim finally went home at 3 A.M. but he couldn't sleep that night, nor the next. He felt such a failure. The medical people so efficiently went about their work. The police quietly and efficiently gathered the needed information. But he—he had none of their professionalism, none of their assured efficiency as he bungled his job as the spiritual father who was to give light and ease pain.

He was surprised, then, when two days later he received a call from the parents of the two dead teenagers asking him to come that evening to the wake. They met him at the door of the funeral parlor. As they led him down the long corridor to the room where the two were, Father Jim could hear whispered comments: "Oh, he must be the priest." "Yes, he's the one." The shattered parents had told many of the young priest who so shared their shock and grief that all he could do was blurt out a ragged sentence and weep with them. They wanted him to lead the funeral the next day.

Paul had told us that "the foolishness of God is wiser than man's wisdom" (1 Cor 1:25). Now James tells us that "the wisdom that comes from heaven is . . . full of mercy and good fruit" (3:17). There are many times in our lives when we are confronted with another's pain, anger, abysmal grief. There seems to be nothing we can humanly say or do. It is a time for being, being with, a time of mercy and compassion. In the end nothing is as supportive as knowing that someone is really with us in our agony. Jim had thought if he were more practiced he might have had a proper "professional" response for these traumatized parents. Perhaps some theological insight could have "made sense" of what had happened. But in fact the young priest, in his need leaning on the Spirit, learned a lifetime lesson: Divine wisdom may seem humanly foolish but it is merciful, it is compassionate—and it is the only response adequate to the great moments of life.

Faith Is the Key

Text: 1 Peter 1

I am sitting here, facing one of the greatest challenges of my life. I open the Bible and turn to the first letter of Peter. I readily identify with this wonderful person, both in his robust, blustery youth and in the gentle concerns of his declining years. Perhaps he has some good advice for me at this time.

"Praise be to the God and Father of our Lord Jesus Christ . . . new birth into a living hope . . . an inheritance that can never perish . . . kept in heaven." For whom? For the one who is shielded by God's power through *faith*.

"In this you greatly rejoice (Do I? Why?) though now for a little while you may have had to suffer grief in all kinds of trials." Yes, it is "a little while" in the light of eternity. And there is a reason for all of this: that my faith may be proved and may result in praise, glory, and honor. For whom? God? Or me? Actually both of us. This is the wonder of God's plan. His glory in creation he has placed in our glory.

Things make a little more sense now.

"Though you have not seen him, you love him"—yes, yes! "And even though you do not see him now, you believe in him."

Yes, *faith is the key*.

I don't know if I can quite say I am "filled with an inexpressible and glorious joy" but there is deep down a peace and a joy, knowing I am receiving the goal of my faith, the salvation of my soul.

Yes, "Praise be to the God and Father of our Lord Jesus Christ!"

Man of His People

Text: 1 Peter 3:6ff

Peter is still a man of his own people, a Jew of the Jews. He frequently quotes the Psalms and the Prophets, the pithy wisdom of the Proverbs. He looks to his mother, Sarah, the wife of his father, Abraham.

And yet he reaches out in all directions to God's elect: Pontus, Galatia, Cappadocia, Asia and Bithynia. He knows that now they are all one people, the people of God.

He is the disciple of his Master. Jesus' own images crop up everywhere. The good news impregnates his teaching.

The big difference we notice, though, is a remarkable mellowness, a gentleness. We would never expect the sword-swinging bravado of Gethsemani to be telling us, "Submit yourself for the Lord's sake to every authority instituted among men" (2:13)—even traffic cops. Submission is a recurring theme in this short letter—time-conditioned though the applications may sometimes be. He uses images we might more expect from mothers. He speaks of sympathy, compassion, and humility. We are to bless the one who insults us. We are to respond with gentleness and respect.

The end is near for Peter. He has indeed matured and is bearing the rich fruits of the Spirit: love, joy, peace, patience, kindness, gentleness (Gal 5:22).

He knows whereof he speaks when he says to us: "Cast all your anxiety on him because he cares for you" (5:7).

The Glorious Past

Text: 2 Peter 1

Peter sat alone in his prison. His "son Mark" attended him when he could. But for the most part he was alone, alone with thoughts and memories. And one great memory enlightened all his darkness: "we were with him on the sacred mountain" (1:18).

A certain luminosity still hovers over Tabor. Mercifully spared of tourist buses—it is too steep for them—it remains a sanctuary of deep prayer. And for Peter it remained the ground of his faith and his teaching: "We did not tell you cleverly invented stories when we told you about the power and coming of our Lord Jesus Christ, but we were eyewitnesses of his majesty . . . we ourselves heard this voice that came from heaven" (1:16ff).

Peter does not have much more time. The Lord has made it known to him (1:14). But this Father of the Church feels "it is right to refresh our memories as

102

long as he lives in the tent of this body." And after? "I will make every effort to see that after my departure you will always be able to remember these things."

And so the old man writes, and continues to write in this second letter. And like Paul, he shows special concern for the elders, those who must carry on the work of leading and guiding the Church.

But all the fire is not yet gone out of this elder. Perhaps it was the recollection of the Lord's own violence at Sodom and Gomorrah, but he is soon using the salty language we might expect from the Peter of old: brute beasts, creatures of instinct, born only to be caught and destroyed . . . an accursed brood!

It does our hearts good to hear them. We only hope we are not among those who deserve them!

Hope Beyond the Holocaust

Text: 2 Peter 3:3ff

Peter, the universal Father of the Church, the first Pope as we would say, is conscious of his obligation to help God's people understand revelation and to bring peace to their hearts. God spoke powerfully through Paul, the apostle of the Gentiles. But "his letters contain some things that are hard to understand" (3:16). They have caused some confusion and concern. Paul was aware of it, especially in regard to the "last days," and sought in some of his letters to clear up the matter and head off exaggerations (see especially 2 Thessalonians—we still find lots of confusion and distortion on this matter today). Now Peter puts his pen to the matter, assuring his readers that his teaching differs in no way from Paul's.

This was certainly a preoccupation with the early Church just as it is today with some preachers and some particular churches. "The end of all things is near"—Peter himself said it (1 Pet 4:7). But now Peter reminds his flock: "Do not forget this one thing, dear friends: With the Lord a day is like a thousand years, and a thousand years are like a day" (3:8). We really do not know the day or the hour. The signs in many ways are always upon us.

But Peter's description of the last times are particularly poignant for our times. They seem, although they were written nearly two thousand years ago, to describe graphically a nuclear holocaust: "The heavens will disappear with a roar; the ele-

103

ments will be destroyed by fire, and the earth and everything in it will be laid bare. . . . That day will bring about the destruction of the heavens by fire, and the elements will melt in the heat" (3:10ff). It is frightening.

Yet without pausing so much as for a breath, Peter goes on: "We are looking forward to a new heaven and a new earth" (3:13). He, our God and Savior, has promised it, a home for the righteous. Even if in our folly and malice we do destroy this home which the Lord has made for us here on earth, it is not the end for those who have thrown in their lot with the Lord. "The Lord's patience means salvation."

What person of Christian instinct does not hope with every fiber of his being that this horrible destruction can be averted? But for the Christian there is hope even beyond the holocaust.

===================================== **Love Me, Love Mine**

Text: 1 John 1

They surrounded him with something like awe, certainly the veneration due a saint. They knew his story, and he never tired of telling it: he had seen the Lord, he had touched the Lord. More, he had even rested his head on the very bosom of the Lord and heard the beating of his heart. He was the first to follow the Lord; he never left the Lord but followed him to the cross. He may not have yet died for the Lord as had the others of that chosen band, but that wasn't his fault. For evidently the Lord wanted him to remain until he came, or at least for a while longer.

But as the saintly old man moved among them—so the Fathers tell us—he no longer spoke much of all these things. He had but one word, a word of life. He never ceased repeating: Children, love one another. And when asked why this was all he had to say, he would reply: He who loves his brother does everything.

These three precious, albeit short, letters certainly confirm the validity of this story. John was indeed the disciple of love. Just count how many times that word is on his pen in these letters.

For him Christianity was clear and simple: "This is the message you have heard from the beginning: We should love one another" (3:11). "Whoever loves his brother lives in the light, and there is nothing in him to make him stumble" (2:10).

But what is love? "This is how we know what love is: Jesus Christ laid down his life for us. And we ought to lay down our lives for our brothers" (3:16).

So simple. So complete. So totally demanding. "But if we love each other, God lives in us and his love is made complete in us" (4:12).

The Disciple Whom Jesus Loved

Text: 2 John

It was many, many years after Jesus had disappeared from the sight of his human eyes and ascended into heaven. He had gazed long and lovingly after him. But life went on and the angels and the Spirit sent him on his way. Still he would always describe himself as "the disciple whom Jesus loved." That was the whole meaning of his life.

It is something to be loved by another. And when that one is the one whom we most love, the one whose love we want more than anything else in this world, then that love defines our lives. We want to so live as to be worthy of that love.

John was so loved. And so he knew the value of love. And he never ceased preaching it.

He was clear on what true love, in fact, is. He had learned it from the Master. "And this is love: that we walk in obedience to his commands" (6). And his command is precisely this: "Walk in love."

But love is discerning. It is not blind. Every virtue, even love, is moderated by prudence.

We are startled at first when we hear this man of love telling a Christian community not to welcome certain people. "Do not take him into your house" (10). There is a special reason for this. In the social context of the time, such a welcome would most likely be interpreted as sponsoring the guest if he began to preach. Therefore the Church could ill afford to welcome one who would teach false doctrine or sow dissension. "Anyone who welcomes him shares in his wicked work" (11).

But this is not John's last word on hospitality. Read the next letter.

Text: 3 John

If true love does call for discernment so that sometimes we are not to welcome others, that is certainly the exceptional situation. Christian love does mean love, support, encouragement, an open-hearted hospitality for friend and stranger alike.

Gaius knew how to show it—even to strangers. And he "sent them on their way in a manner worthy of God" (6).

As is so often the case, the good stand out even more in contrast to the opposite. Yes, even in the early Church, while an apostle still walked the earth, there were these contrasts among the people of God. There are the malicious gossipers who do not welcome and do not let others welcome.

"Dear friend, do not imitate what is evil but what is good" (11). John's advice is as simple as that.

These three letters of John are quite short, among the shortest in the New Testament. But this lover is impatient with this mode of communication. He much prefers the more fully human, face to face communication. We glean what we can from them, and find so much between the lines.

LETTER OF JUDE

A Holy Zealotry

Text: Jude

Zealots see black and white, nature and grace, the godly and the ungodly. The lines are sharply drawn for them. About the ungodly nothing good can be said.

Jude is of this ilk. Not only does he indict the ungodly ones of every possible moral depravity, he identifies them with every evil character that has appeared in Sacred Scripture from beginning to end: Cain, the Egyptians, Balaam, Korah . . . His pique rises to eloquence in the many images he employs: "clouds without rain, blown along by the wind; autumn trees, without fruit and uprooted—twice dead; wild waves of the sea, foaming up their shame; wandering stars, for whom the blackest darkness has been reserved forever." Magnificent! Awesome! And frightening, in its possible consequences, if he had not written on.

When Jude comes to advise his flock on how to respond to these ungodly ones, we see the marks of *holy* zealotry—one that is of God. His advice is all positive: build up . . . keep in love . . . be merciful . . . reach out to others (20ff). There is no self-righteous crusader here.

We don't know much about Jude—who he really is. Is he one of the Twelve? I think he would be a man around whom it might be a bit difficult to live. He surely would keep us on our toes, keep some of the zip in our Christian lives, keep us growing. We need some "holy zealotry" in our church communities.

REVELATION

== **In a Cave**

Text: Revelation 1

The sun, hot and strong, picked out the white stone houses that lined the road as it climbed, zigzag, up the hill. If anything the buildings were too white, like those in a travel agent's brochure. At the top, in full command, was the medieval fortress-monastery of Saint John. I was happy I did not have to climb all the way to the top this day. Already the perspiration trickled down my back, soaking my shirt.

I had been to the monastery, for on this ecumenical visit I was the guest of the Exarch of Patmos. This morning, though, I was seeking out the cave that was hidden off the road about halfway up the hill. There were no signs to point it out. Few pilgrims come to Patmos. And the monks are not eager to attract tourists to the sacred spot.

I slipped into the cool quiet, settled on the natural seat in the wall of the cave, and let my eyes adjust to the diminished light before opening my Bible. The seat was very smooth—many had sat upon it, even, according to tradition, the author of the Book of Revelation. For this was "Saint John's Cave."

With a fervent prayer and relying on the intercession of the author, I began to read this book which had always been for me a sealed book. That day sparks leapt out, and I was grateful for each one of them.

I think, in some ways, Revelation is a book to be read rather more passively, letting the visions rise and fall, one after the other. We should not expect to understand all. In fact, we should be grateful if we are brought into the secret of any one of them. It is an ongoing challenge, a book that will always have more to say to us. Indeed that is true of every book of Scripture. Maybe the obviousness of it in John's book at the end of the Bible is a good reminder for us that this is so.

This is "the revelation of Jesus Christ" (1:1). The lover of Christ will search it again and again in his eagerness to catch any new insight into the wonder and glory of his Beloved. The New Testament began with the story of Jesus' human-

glory of his Beloved. The New Testament began with the story of Jesus' humanity—all too human, abased even to a shameful death—and offered only the least glimpses of his glory. Now rays of that glory are allowed to shine through in sign and symbol and we find them baffling, astounding, in many ways incomprehensible. They entice, and promise ever more.

The freedom of Patmos (prison can be a very free place for the spiritual person) enabled John to be a true seer—a see-er. This record of his revelations invites us to share in his vision.

Knock, Knock

Text: Revelation 3:14ff

The story is well known. A famous artist, inspired by Revelation 3:20, painted a picture of Jesus standing at a door knocking. When the finished work was displayed, sharp-eyed critics were quick to jump on him: There was no handle on the door. Replied the artist: Of course not. The door of the soul can only be opened from within.

That is certainly true. No one respects us as fully as does our God. He made us, and he knows the greatest thing about us is our freedom—for therein lies our power to love. He respects our freedom and he will never push his way into our lives. He stands respectfully at the door and knocks: Knock, knock.

If we open, he will come in. What a beautiful picture he paints—two friends together at an intimate meal, and not even across the table from each other, but side by side, so that we can rest our heads on his bosom as did the disciple whom he loves.

And to such a victor he promises that this is only the beginning (some victory—all we had to do was open the door). We will sit with him on his throne, one with him and the Father, forever.

But the thing that strikes me the most in this powerful message to the church of Laodicea is this:

Our Lord begins the message by being very frank: you are neither hot nor cold. And he, who was always burning with love to do the will of the Father, experiences a natural revulsion: "I am about to spit you out of my mouth" (3:16). And it is to these very ones, those whom he finds so naturally repugnant, that he says: "Here I am! I stand at the door and knock" (3:20). So great is his love that it cuts right through his natural feelings and totally overcomes them.

What was it that John wrote in his first letter? "This is how we know what love is: Jesus Christ laid down his life for us" (3:16)—yes, even when we are disgusting sinners.

Text: Revelation 5:5

I slipped out of my sandals and walked gingerly into the mosque. I have always found mosques lightsome and airy, pervaded by the Spirit, a climate of prayer. In the noise of cities, I prefer them as a place to meditate.

The thick pile of the magnificent rug felt good between my toes. I settled down not far from a young man absorbed in his devotions. He bobbed up and down. His whole being was part of his prayer. Then I could hear his murmuring. He was in the midst of a favored devotion of the sons of Islam; he was reciting the hundred names of Allah. As I listened, there came to my mind the fifth verse of this chapter in Revelation: "The Lion of the tribe of Judah, the Root of David."

My Moslem brother could well understand these titles of the Lord. In fact, we were now in prayer together in the Dome of the Rock, one of the three holiest places for the Moslem, the great mosque built on the site of the great Temple of Solomon. Here in the heart of Judah David had, at divine direction, first established this holy of holies. As the young Moslem continued his prayer I thought of how we, too, could glean from the Book of Revelation, if not a hundred names, nonetheless many rich and beautiful ones that can invite us to enter ever more deeply into the mystery of Christ.

Let us recall some of them:

The faithful witness, the firstborn from the dead, the ruler of the kings of the
    earth (1:5)
The Alpha and the Omega (1:8)
Who is, and who was, and who is to come (1:8)
The First and the Last (1:17)
The Living One (1:18)
Who died and came to life again (2:8)
The Son of God (2:18)
He who is holy and true (3:7)
He who holds the key of David (3:7)
The Lord God Almighty (4:8)
The Lion of the tribe of Judah, the Root of David (5:5)
The Lamb who was slain (5:12)
Sovereign Lord, holy and true (6:10)

The Beginning and the End (22:13)
The Offspring of David, and the Bright Morning Star (22:16)

Make your own list. Question them: What's in a name? What do they tell us of him? Let them sit in your mind until they form your heart, and then let your whole being respond in and through them.

Star Wars

Text: Revelation 12:7ff

"Wars and rumors of war"—here is where it all began: Satan, "who leads the whole world astray," encounters Michael and his angels. "And there was war in heaven" (12:7). This whole center section of the Book of Revelation is one of battle and conflict, of the most ferocious struggle between good and evil.

The imagery is wild, and frightening at times. Eastern mythology has had its own images, so fierce and so brightly colored that they tend to amuse us. Our imagery today is that of star wars, with Darth Vadar and other sinister characters. But the reality is always the same: the age-old conflict between evil and good. Satan rose against God. Cain slew Abel. And John lives in the midst of another life and death struggle: Rome, mighty Rome, seeks to strangle and annihilate that poor little sect called the Disciples of the Way, or Christians. The struggle had a long way to go, and indeed it still goes on if we see Rome as the "world"—"the cravings of sinful man, the lust of his eyes and the boasting of what he has and does" (1 Jn 2:16). But the Lord does not will the death of the sinful, but rather that they be converted and live. Rome, the great Babylon, might seem to fall, but rather she will rise and become the Eternal City, the center of Christianity.

A key role in this ultimate battle is played by a woman "clothed with the sun, with the moon under her feet and a crown of twelve stars on her head" (12:1). In the mysterious chronology of prophecy her end is presented before her beginning. First she will fulfill her role to give birth to "a male child, who will rule the nations with an iron scepter" (12:5). It is he who will lead us all to the final victory. And to her will there ever be paid special honor for what she suffered in mothering the Savior of all humankind.

115

Text: Revelation 19:6ff

By this time your head may well be reeling. Image upon image upon image—enough to make the most fantastic Hindu or Buddhist temple look rather mild. Just try to conjure up the locusts or the horses described in chapter nine!

What are we supposed to do with all of this? Talk about distractions in prayer! John explains very few of his images, either explicitly or implicitly. He has given ample material for preachers' fancies until indeed all are fulfilled. Come, Lord Jesus. Don't put that off too long, for we have had already enough and more than enough of wild speculation and congregation rousing. The end has come and gone so many times in the imaginations of your zealous preachers.

It is not all that clear what we as individuals can profitably do with much of the imagery in this Book of Revelation. At best we listen quietly and hope the Spirit will deign to speak to us in a meaningful way through it.

But there is one very precious element in this book which we can most profitably use, and that is its rich hymnody. What a rich school of praise, from the transmission of the heavenly hymn

Holy, holy, holy
is the Lord God Almighty,
who was and is and is to come.
You are worthy, our Lord and God,
to receive glory and honor and power,
for you created all things,
and by your will they were created
and have their being (4:8ff)

to the final hymn of triumph

Hallelujah!
For our Lord God Almighty reigns.
Let us rejoice and be glad
and give him glory!

For the wedding of the Lamb has come,
and his bride has made herself ready.
Fine linen, bright and clean,
was given her to wear (19:6ff).

Undoubtedly, John has drawn from the repertoire of the Christian community of his time, though some may be hymns that come, as it were, directly from the heavenly choirs. They offer us, especially at this time when the Church is renewing her liturgy, a veritable storehouse of rich and beautiful material.

The individual can well use them, too, in personal devotion. They form a wonderful school of praise. There is perhaps no area of prayer in which we are weaker than that of praise. These hymns, even as we pray them, can form our minds and hearts and open them to the wonders of God, calling forth torrents of praise. We will come to know in truth that he is "King of kings and Lord of lords."

"Let us rejoice and be glad and give him glory! For the wedding of the Lamb has come and his bride has made herself ready" (19:7).

The tone of these last chapters of John's revelations are very different—praise, joy, glory, light, expectation. The end, the fulfillment is near. "Come, I will show you the bride."

The bridal image is found throughout the Old and New Testament. Israel was the bride of God, so often unfaithful. He made his prophet the foolish lover of a harlot, to show the folly of his own love. He inspired a wildly erotic love song to try to convey his own love. In the new covenant marriage was raised to the power of a sacrament, a special vehicle of grace, to symbolize the fidelity of his own complete and unending devotion to his Church. Now we are told of the fulfillment of that sacrament. "Come, I will show you the bride, the wife of the Lamb" (21:9).

"Blessed are those who are invited to the supper of the Lamb" (19:9). Heaven is to be a great marriage feast, when the Church, all of us, the faithful, will enter into the house of our Beloved and be forever most intimately one with him in the most ravishing embraces of love. What better image can be used for what eye has not seen, nor ear heard, what is beyond human imagination?

"I am making everything new," says the Lord—"a new heaven and a new earth." Peter looked forward to it. John has seen it!

Creation has gone full circle. We are back to the first days in Eden, when God came down in the cool of the evening and walked arm in arm with Adam. But where sin abounded, grace abounds still more. An even more complete and intimate union has been prepared for us by the Lamb who was slain, a oneness with him, with the divine, that is beyond our comprehension.

"Amen. Come, Lord Jesus."